OPEN UNIVERSITY
Student Support Services

Dr. J. Prasanth Kumar
M.A., M.Ed., M.Phil., Ph.D.
A. L. College of Education
Guntur–522 002 (Andhra Pradesh)

Editors
Dr. Digumarti Bhaskara Rao
M.Sc., M.A., M.A., M.Ed., Ph.D.
R.V.R. College of Education
D-43, S.V.N. Colony
Guntur–522 006 (Andhra Pradesh)

Mr. Garimella Sundara Rao
M.Sc., M.Ed.
A. L. College of Education
Guntur–522 002 (Andhra Pradesh)

DISCOVERY PUBLISHING HOUSE
NEW DELHI–110 002

First Published–2000
Reprinted 2011

ISBN 81-7141-550-4

Published by :
Discovery Publishing House
4831/24, Ansari Road, Prahlad Street
Darya Ganj, New Delhi–110 002 (INDIA)
Phone : 3279245
Fax.: 91-11-3253475

Laser Typeset by :

Allied Computers
Karnal (Haryana)

Mehra Offset Press
Delhi

Preface

The concept of Open University is a philosophical concept providing an open access to higher education for all those who could not or did not join the formal educational stream. The first Indian Open University—Andhra Pradesh Open University, now it is called Dr. B. R. Ambedkar Open University—came into existence on 26th August, 1982 being disclosing a new vista of possibilities in Indian education.

The students of open learning need support services in order to overcome barriers of learning which result from the loneliness of the students working on their own. Identifying the importance of student support services of an open university, the attitudes of academic counsellors and learners of the first Indian open university towards the student support services were studied. The results are quite interesting. This study will help many researchers and academicians in studying and improving the quality of student support services of open universities and distance education institutions.

We are grateful to Dr. K. Jagannadha Rao and Dr. T. J. Rajendra Prasad for their effective guidance in completing this study successfully. We are thankful to the chiefs of the study centres, academic counsellors and students of Dr. B. R. Ambedkar Open University for their continuous co-operation in data collection.

—J. Prasanth Kumar
—D. Bhaskara Rao
—G. Sundara Rao

Contents

1
Introduction

Higher education is of paramount importance. It provides and supplies a wide range of sophisticated man power needed for the development of individual. The citizens always look for attainment of individual progress by joining the system. This is reflected in the aspirations of the people for enrichment of social prestige, achievement of high rate of mobility, attainment of economic gains and improvement of individual's knowledge and skills over several aspects of daily life. While intending to cater to the development needs of the society and of individuals, the higher education system aspires for practicing democratic norms. It is expected that the system must be accessible to an optimum level of those citizens who are capable of pursuing higher studies. In this context, the University Education Commission (1948–49) remarked: "In a well planned educational system opportunities will be provided at every level to the pupils for the exercise of their reflective powers, artistic abilities and practical work." Further, the Commission opined that "our system must provide for every young person, education to the extent that he can profit from it...". These ideas acted as influential factors in expansion of higher education in the country.

Moreover, the pressure on higher education has been increasing due to rising social aspirations of the masses. Keeping in view the popular demand for higher education, the political forces of different regions have played a major role in enhancement of facilities for higher education in different parts of the country. As a result, during post-independence period, a tremendous increase was marked in terms of establishment of substantial number of higher education institutions in different states. At the time of independence, there were 19 universities with enrolment of 1.8 lakh students. At present there are 150 universities with 33 lakh students (University Hand Book, 1985–86). The increasing trend of students enrolment and number of universities shows the interest of our country in university education. Taking into consideration the factor of increasing rate of enrolment in higher education, it could be guessed that the massive entrance would augment the administrative as well as financial burden of the system. Hence, to avoid increasing administrative and financial burdens and to maintain academic standards of the formal system, it was thought appropriate to divert the overflow of entrance through creation of alternative channels of higher education.

Moreover, owing to certain inherent limitations, the formal system cannot act as a viable means for higher studies of those who are capable enough to study but belonged to the regions far away from the institutions, lacked motivation to continue with formal stream, belonged to upper age group, took employment at the end of schooling, found the formal system expensive and discontinued for one or other reasons and could not take up the opportunity to pursue education as youngsters etc. These limitations marked in the formal system paved the way for encouragement of parallel streams of higher education. In these contexts, during 1960, the Planning Commission of India had pointed out, "In addition to provision in the plan for expansion of facilities for higher education, proposals for evening colleges, correspondence courses and the award of external degrees are at present under consideration" (Planning Commission, 1960–65).

On the basis of observation made by the Planning Commission (1960–65) the matter of creation of alternative channels of higher education was brought to the consideration of Central Advisory Board of Education (CABE). In its 28th meeting (1961) a resolution was passed for opening the avenue of correspondence education at university level. Subsequently, the Ministry of Education, Government of India constituted an Expert Committee (1961) consisting ten members from different organizations such as University Grants Commission, Ministry of Education and some selected universities. In its recommendations, the Expert Committee highlighted several issues pertinent to correspondence education such as flexibility in the system, institutions of correspondence education and universities, instructional process, teachers, introduction of courses from Arts, Commerce, Science and Technology fields, duration of courses etc. The Committee during the deliberations suggested that as a pilot project correspondence education may be introduced at the University of Delhi.

Creation of Correspondence Institution (1962)

The University of Delhi agreed to the proposal made by the Expert Committee on Correspondence Education. As a result, during 1962 it came out with its School of Correspondence Courses and Continuing Education. In the initial stage the institute restricted its programme to Arts courses at undergraduate level.

Recommendations of the Education Commission (1964–66)

The success that University of Delhi achieved in opening the correspondence institute seems to have encouraged the Education Commission (1964–66) to recommend in favour of correspondence education in the country. The Education Commission has recommended, "The opportunities for part time education through programmes like correspondence courses should be expanded as widely as possible and should also include courses in Science and Technology."

Growth of Correspondence Institutions in India

The recommendations and observations of the above committees, paved the way for the introduction of correspondence courses in other universities consequently. During 1968 and 1969 four universities instituted Directorates of Correspondence Courses viz., Punjab (1968), Rajasthan (1968), Mysore (1969) and Meerut (1969).

The rapid expansion of correspondence education took place during 1970–71 to 1977–78. At present more than 40 universities offer correspondence education at various levels. Mostly in India the correspondence education institutes are named as the Directorates of Correspondence Education and are affiliated to conventional universities.

In these Directorates the admission procedures, curriculum and examinations are mostly similar to formal education. As a result, only a section of left out population is absorbed by the correspondence education. Keeping in view some of the rigidities in correspondence education, a flexible type of education is necessary to absorb all the aspirants to higher education at different levels.

Hence another form of Open Learning System has been introduced naming as Distance Education through Open University system of education.

The Concept of Distance Education

It is only during the last few decades, with the beginning of the British Open University in England, that distance education emerged as a concept different from correspondence education. Distance educators themselves took many years to finally realize that they were more than correspondence educators—it was during the Twelfth World Conference of the International Council for Correspondence Education held at Vancouver in 1982 that the Council was renamed as the International Council for Distance Education.

History of Distance Education

The general belief so far has been that the modern history of correspondence instruction began in 1840 with Issac Pitman's Shorthand Course for distance students through the Penny post. However, some researchers have traced the forerunners of the distance education of to-day to 1833 when a private teacher of English taught composition by post providing the two-way communication which is the predominant characteristic of distance education. In 1856, a School of Modern Languages established by Langenscheidt and Toussaint started teaching foreign languages through correspondence. In the USA, the first efforts to organise correspondence instruction were made in 1873. Later on, the idea of a land grant college with a campus extending to the state boundaries resulted in the establishment of correspondence courses in some universities in 1890. Although correspondence education played only a limited role in the formal secondary school system, colleges and universities in the USA, it has been more extensive in the States than in any other country. In Europe, pioneering work was done in Germany and Sweden in 1890 with the establishment of Fern Lchrinstitut in Berlin and Hermods in Sweden. With the onset of twentieth century, a number of correspondence instruction schools were set up throughout Europe.

Varied names such as home study, postal tuition, correspondence courses, independent study, etc., were given to the earlier forms of distance education programmes throughout the world. Even now terms like off-campus studies, external studies, non-formal education, etc., continue to be in use of these the term correspondence education has widely been accepted. All these terms were essentially associated with non-traditional teaching-learning programmes, which had many similarities. In the beginning print medium was the source. But in due course of time the progressive institutions brought in the multi-media approach in their teaching/learning system.

This development raised doubts in some minds about the appropriateness of the term correspondence education and generated thinking for finding a broader and more appropriate term for this innovative and non-traditional teaching/learning system. This issue was finally clinched at the 12th World Conference held in Vancouver, Canada in 1982 under the Presidency of Prof. Bakhshish Singh and the International Council for Distance Education (ICDE) was renamed as International Council for Distance Education (ICDE). Since then the term Distance Education has been (catching up) popular in all countries.

What is Distance Education?

Distance Education has been defined by several writers like Wedemeyer, Holmberg, Moore, Peters and Keegan, each emphasising certain aspects of the system. It is, however, to the credit of Desmond Keegan that he has attempted a synthesis of most of the definitions.

Definition

According to Desmond Keegan :

— The quasi-permanent separation of teacher and learner throughout the length of the learning process, this distinguishes it from conventional face-to-face education.

— The influence of an educational organization both in planning and preparation of learning materials and in the provision of student support services; this distinguishes it from private study and teach yourself programmes.

— The use of technical media, print, audio, video or computer, to unite teacher and learner and carry the content of the course.

— The provision of two-way communication so that the student may benefit or even initiate a dialogue; this distinguishes it from other uses of technology in education.

— The quasi-permanent absence of a learning group throughout the length of the learning process so that people are usually taught as individuals and not in groups, with the possibility of occasional meeting for both didactic and socialisation purposes.

Distance Education Abroad

It is very difficult to trace the history of correspondence education in the world. For, in several countries it originated in different forms and at different times to meet the needs of those countries. It can be said that the idea originated in the 19th century when in some European countries institutions were established to undertake coaching external students reading for a degree or otherwise. However, it was during the 30s of this century that correspondence education system took deep roots in several countries. The founding of the International Council of Correspondence Education in 1938 is indicative of the fact that the idea caught the attention of the educationists throughout the world. We shall examine the growth of correspondence education in a few developed and developing countries.

In Australia, the 1909 Act of Parliament which established the University of Queensland contained a provision for external studies. It enabled all adult of mature age to gain entry into university education by study through correspondence. Five of the nineteen universities in Australia to-day offer distance teaching facility.

In Russia, there are 14 distance teaching universities and about 100 departments or divisions in the "other institutions of higher learning offering courses through distance teaching."

In USA, education through correspondence started in the Universities of Chicago as early as 1891. Later, several universities and colleges started correspondence programmes. In recent years, a number of institutions were established offering educational opportunities for adult learners who are home-based and work-based.

In Kenya, the Institute of Adult Studies, University College, Nairobi, was established in 1967 on the recommendations of the Kenyan Education Commission.

The first open university was established in the United Kingdom in 1969. It was established mainly to teach adult students who are at a distance. After a good deal of preparatory work, it started enrolling students from 1971.

According to Indira Gandhi National Open University Project Report, September, 1985, the following are the Open Universities in the world.

Table 1.1: Open Universities in the World

Sl. No.	*Name of University*	*Date of Incorporation*
1.	Open University, Milton Keynes, United Kingdom	1969
2.	Universidad Nacional de Education a Distancia, Madrid, Spain	1972
3.	Free University of Iran, Tehran, Iran	1973
4.	Fern Universitat, Hagen, Federal Republic of Germany	1974
5.	Everyman's University, Tel Aviv, Israel	1974

Contd.

Table 1.1: Contd.

Sl. No.	Name of University	Date of Incorporation
6.	Allama Iqbal Open University, Islamabad, Pakistan	1974
7.	Athabasca University, Edmonton, Alberta, Canada	1975
8.	Universided Nacional Abierta, Carcas, Venezuela	1977
9.	Universidad Estatal a Distancia, San Jose, Costa Rica	1977
10.	Sukhothai Thammathirat Open University, Bangkok, Thailand	1978
11.	Central Broadcasting & Television University, Beijing, China and 28 T.A. Universities	1978
12.	Open University of Sri Lanka, Nawala, Nugegoda, Sri Lanka	1981
13.	Open University, Heerlen, Netherlands	1981
14.	University of Air, Japan	1982
15.	Andhra Pradesh Open University, Hyderabad, Andhra Pradesh, India	1982
16.	Korea Air and Correspondence University, Seoul, Korea	1983
17.	National Open University, Abuja, Nigeria	1983
18.	Universitas Terbuka, Indonesia	1984
19.	Indira Gandhi National Open University, New Delhi	1985

We shall now deal with the Open Universities established in some of the Asian countries. In Pakistan, an Open University was established in 1974.

China has a long tradition of correspondence education imparted by regular educational institutions in recent times, during the early 1960s.

Thailand established the Sukhothai Thammathirat Open University in September 1978 to democratise higher education and to supplement educational opportunities provided by the conventional universities.

Most of the distance teaching institutions in different parts of the world were established to meet the immediate and long-term needs of higher education. But a feature which is common to all the countries is their emphasis on correspondence teaching. Though in a few countries other media like Radio and T.V. are also being used, this did not reduce the importance of effectiveness of correspondence tuition. In recent years, with the development of communication technology, full-fledged universities, popularly called open universities, are being established in several countries to strengthen distance teaching using diverse devices in an integrated manner.

The importance of distance teaching, whatever be the institutional arrangement, is increasing everywhere. As the need and demand for higher education increases and as the new educational and communication technologies are becoming available, every country finds it desirable and even convenient to start an open university than merely add a conventional-type university. This indeed is the urge behind the establishment of open universities.

The Concept of an Open University

The concept of an Open University is new. The Open University system is not just a multimedia approach to teaching distant learner. It is a philosophical concept of providing open access to higher education for all those disadvantaged groups who could not or did not join the formal stream. It aims to equalise educational opportunities. It aims to equalise educational opportunities. It aims to train people in various arts and crafts to develop their skills in different jobs. It is different from the conventional university system in several respects. Its objectives, its operations, and its spatial needs lend it a very distinctive character. Besides doing away with the conventional restrictions of place, time and entry qualifications, it seeks to democratise higher education.

Genesis of Open University System in India

In India, the proposal for establishing an Open University

was initiated in seventies. The Ministry of Education and Social Welfare in collaboration with Ministry of Information and Broadcasting, and the UGC, organised a seminar in December 1970 for the observance of International Year of Education. Inaugurating the seminar, Prof. V.K.R.V. Rao, the then Education Minister, first mooted the idea of establishing an Open University in India and observed:

> "...It must cover not only the comparatively limited number of university students, but should cover much larger number of students who drop out from the school at various points, the neo-literates, and eventually all adults who desire to avail these programmes of continuing education...The new interesting programmes of instruction, based on modern science-oriented educational technology for students of higher education studying in the Open University should be made available to this much larger body of population which remains outside the so-called university system."

In the same year that the Union Ministry of Education organised a seminar under the Chairmanship of Prof. D.S. Kothari with its participants drawn from the UNESCO and several countries including the UK, USA and Japan. As a result of suggestion from the seminar, the Government of India appointed a working group with Mr. G. Parthasarathy the then Vice-Chancellor of Jawaharlal Nehru University, Delhi, in 1971 to examine the feasibility of establishing an Open University in India. This working group in its report stated:

> In a situation of this type, where the expansion of enrolments in higher education has to continue at a terrific pace and where available resources in terms of men and money are limited, the obvious solution, if proper standards are to be maintained and the demand for higher education from different sections of the people is to be met, is to adopt the Open University system with its provision of higher education of part-time or own time basis. The group, therefore, recommends that the Government of India should establish, as early as possible, a National Open University by an Act of Parliament.

The report of the Working Group was submitted in 1975 and some spade work was done to establish a National Open University.

First Open University at the State Level

At the State level, in 1978 the then Education Minister of Andhra Pradesh Sri Bhavanam Venkatram came to evince a keen interest in the concept of Open University. He asked Prof. Ram Reddy, the then Vice-Chancellor of Osmania University, who was scheduled to go to the UK, to visit the British Open University and submit a report. On his return from England, Prof. Ram Reddy gave him a note on its significant features. But as there had been no tangible governmental move in that regard, it was proposed to set up an autonomous College of Education to be run by Osmania University. The proposal was accepted by the University's Syndicate and a Committee was appointed to consider its feasibility. At the instance of Osmania University a consultancy report was prepared by Mr. Greville Rumble. As per this report the proposed college was to introduce the distance education system with its successful students receiving their Degrees to be awarded by the Osmania University.

While the work on this project was going on, there was a change in the Ministry with the then Education Minister becoming the Chief Minister of the State. He showed a renewed interest in the distance education system and appointed a Committee with Prof. Ram Reddy as its Chairman to study the possibility of starting an Open University. The Committee submitted its report to the Government in August 1982 and a Bill based on it was tabled in the Andhra Pradesh Legislature within a week of the submission of the Report. It was passed in the Legislative Assembly on the 24th of August, 1982 and was approved by the Legislative Council on the following day. Thus the enactment of the bill took place in record time. This was appreciated by all the political parties of the state of its significance to the educational advancement of the people of the State. The Andhra Pradesh Open University was inaugurated by the President of India on the 26th of August, 1982. Prof. Ram Reddy was appointed its Vice-Chancellor on the 18th November, 1982. Thus the first Indian Open University came into being disclosing a new vista of possibilities in Indian Education.

National Open University

At the national level, however, the earlier proposals remained on paper and no action was taken on the Parthasarathy Committee Report and nothing was known about the Draft Bill prepared. The idea was again revived in 1984. The Prime Minister Rajiv Gandhi in his first broadcast to the nation in January 1985 gave expression to this in the form of a policy statement when he announced the establishment of a National Open University as a part of the new educational policy. In pursuance of this, a Committee was constituted by the Ministry of Education with eminent educationists the Committee, apart from preparing a Draft Bill submitted a project report, dealing the various aspects relating to the establishment of National Open University. The Government, committed as it is to strengthen distance education in the country, introduced a Bill in the Parliament immediately. The Indira Gandhi National Open University Bill was passed by both the Houses in August, 1985 and the University came into being on 20th September, 1985. Then Prof. G. Ram Reddy was appointed as Vice-Chancellor who acted as Officer on Special Duty for Expert Committee for the preparation of Project Report. Thus the idea of National Open University initiated in 1970, became a reality in 1985.

The Andhra Pradesh Open University was renamed as Dr. B.R. Ambedkar Open University on the occasion of the centenary birth anniversary of Dr. B.R. Ambedkar in the year 1992.

Aims of Open University System

"Open University" or distance education is viewed as a system which can do away with inequalities in the educational system. This new non-formal system of education which can democratise higher education by providing a second opportunity to all those who were denied it earlier which maintaining high quality in the contents of education.

The Term 'open' Generally Refers to Four Aspects

(a) People, where it would not debar applicants on account of their lack of educational qualifications;

(b) place, in the sense that learning would be home based and not restricted to class room or a campus;

(c) the use of new methods of teaching; and

(d) ideas.

Objectives of the Dr. B. R. Ambedkar Open University

(1) To provide educational opportunities to those who could not, for one reason or another, to take advantage of those offered by the other institutions of higher learning.

(2) To realise equality of educational opportunity for as large a number of people as possible including those in employment, house-wives and other adults who wish to upgrade their education or to acquire knowledge and studies in various fields through distance education.

(3) To provide flexibility with regard to eligibility for enrolment, age of entry, choice of courses, methods of learning, conduct of examinations and implementation of educational programmes.

(4) To formulate programmes complementary to those of existing universities in the State so as to maintain the highest standards on par with those of the best universities in the country.

(5) To promote integration within the State through its policies and programmes.

(6) To offer Degree Courses and Non-Degree Certificate courses for the benefit of the working population in various fields and those who wish to enrich their lives by studying subjects of cultural or aesthetic values.

(7) To make provision for research and for the advancement and dissemination of knowledge.

Organisational Structure of Dr. B.R. Ambedkar Open University

The organizational structure of the university is similar to that of the other universities in the State though a few changes have been made in its structure to suit the character of the university. The Governor of Andhra Pradesh is the ex-officio Chancellor of the University. There is an Executive Council which consists of three categories of members ex-officio, nominated and elected. All the executive authority is vested in the Executive Council. The Academic Council of the University is known as the Academic Planning Board. It is the main body dealing with all policies relating to academic matters. The Vice-Chancellor is the academic and administrative head, he is appointed by the Chancellor from among the names given by a Committee specially appointed for the purpose. The term of the office of the Vice-Chancellor is three years, but he is eligible for another term. There is a provision for the appointment of the Directors who are comparable to the Pro-Vice-Chancellors in other universities. In addition, there are three Registrars, Finance Officer, Deans and Heads of Departments. In all these matters, the provisions of the Act of the Dr. Ambedkar Open University are similar to those other acts in the State.

Instructional Methods

A flexible instructional system is basic to the concept of an Open University. Since most of the Open University students are likely to be employees and house-wives and scattered over a wide area including the interior and remote villages, they may find it inconvenient to be physically present in a classroom for lectures at a stipulated time and place. This inherent limitations make it imperative to explore alternatives and exploit the modern communication technologies for the advantage of the distant learner. Dr. B.R. Ambedkar Open University has adopted an integrated media approach, in the form of print materials, broadcasting and audio-visual aids, supported by tutorial system, contact classes and summer schools. While print materials, the master medium are provided for all courses, the use of other communication media radio, television, audio and video depends on circumstances and the nature of the courses. To-day, radio is within the reach of most of the people, but other means such as video and audio players and television sets are scarce. Such equipment will be installed at the study centres while a television broadcast has the advantage of wide coverage, its time may be inconvenient to the viewer. As against this, a student can use a video player whenever he likes and as often as he wants it.

Student Support Services

To enable the students to have regular contacts with the university, study centres have been established, 85 in number and located in each district of the State and the twin cities of Hyderabad and Secunderabad, including one in Central Jail. In outside the States, Delhi, Chennai and Bangalore cities also study centres are set up. The study centres are located in the existing educational institutions and normally function on all holidays and Sundays and in the evenings on working days.

The diversity of means that the Open University can employ, adequately strengthened by well-organised programmes of counselling and guidance, promises a new era in our educational endeavour, and endeavour in which education is transformed into voluntary creative learning.

The Importance of Student Support in Distance Education

In Open University distance educators have come to recognise that in addition to the specially prepared course material which is now the hallmark of an Open University or Distance Education mode of learning, students, especially in their first years of learning at a distance, need a whole range of different kinds of 'support' if they are to make best use of the wider opportunity that Distance Education offers.

The student support services are to help students to overcome barriers to learning which result from the loneliness of the student working on his own. The barriers are:

Academic Barriers: Even the best prepared course materials contain areas of difficulty, new concepts, theoretical abstractions, densely argued texts. Without any support the student at a distance may feel that he or she cannot manage and given up eventually.

Study Skills Barriers: Serious attention has to be paid to the development of the relevant skills that students need in order to begin to make use of the course materials that they receive.

Institutional Barriers: Learning at a distance involves the student in a wide range of unfamiliar systems with their own problems. These range from the simple non-receipt of course material (whom should the student contact), or lost assignment, to the whole area of how to enable students to make the best use of the multi-media mix that is offered. Students need advice on how they can make choices about which contact sessions to attend, advice about how to learn from distance teaching, and who to turn to for non-academic advice.

To overcome the above barriers the student support services are highly needed and they significantly contribute for the effective realization of the goals of Distance Education.

Study Centre and its Functions

Each study centre is headed by a Deputy Director/Assistant Director/Co-ordinator who arranges contact-cum-counselling programmes for the students admitted into it and avails itself of the services of the members of the staff of local universities/ colleges on part-time basis. The contact programmes are meant for discussion of the study materials supplied to the students, the showing of video films based on their lessons, and the playing of audio tapes to which the students seek guidance from the counsellors with regard to their studies and serve the same purpose as face to face interaction.

Each study centre is provided with a V.C.R. and a T.V. set for the video lessons. It is also supplied audio cassettes in sufficient number for the students to listen to audio lessons. Arrangements are made for the transferring of the radio and audio lessons by the students on to their own tapes if so desired.

The study centre also makes available to its students copies of the radio time-tables indicating the titles of the lessons broadcast by the AIR, Hyderabad on its B transmission. The radio lessons are broadcast five days a week.

Need and Significance of the Study

Dr. B. R. Ambedkar Open University based on the concept of 'Open Learning' the university represents a unique system of realising the democratization of higher education and the ideal of 'continuing education'. The setting up of Dr. B.R.

Ambedkar Open University the first of its kind in the country will go a long way in extending educational opportunities to people in all walks of life without any restriction based on age, sex, occupation or residential situation.

The open university is visualised with great expectations to encourage, strengthen and democratise higher education with flexible methods. Its instruction was through multi-media approach. In this case the success depends mainly on instructional organisation or methods that are in use. The open university keeping in view the characteristics of distance education learners, it has planned a well developed student support services in order to clarify their academic problems. If student support services are not maintained well, the students may face problems to continue with their studies.

For effective meet out of these student support services, Academic Counsellors play an important role through study centres for the benefit of the students. Hence there is a need to take up as study. The Student Support Services of Dr. B.R. Ambedkar Open University.

It is also necessary for assessing the extent to which the student support services are really helping students to overcome their problems for successful completion of their courses.

The Present Study

The investigator would like to take up this study to understand student support services of open university, and to study the attitudes of Academic Staff and Learners who are involved in preparation to disseminating stage of instructional material and perform other functions at study centres in the form of student support services.

Learners are real consumers of the student support services of Open University. It may be appropriate to include them also in the study to measure their attitudes.

Title of the Study

The title of the present study reads as: "A Study of Attitudes of Academic Counsellors and Learners towards the Student Support Services of Dr. B. R. Ambedkar Open University."

Definition of the Terms

Attitude: Attitudes are learned emotionally last pre-dispositions to react in a consistent manner, favourable or unfavourable toward certain objects, people, ideas or situations. A person attitudes are normally inferred from his behaviour and generally cannot be measured as directly as skills or knowledge of facts or concepts. ..."attitudes are selectively acquired and integrated through learning and experience... They are enduring dispositions indicating response consistency...positive or negative effect toward a social or psychological object represents the salient characteristic of an attitude" (Khan & Weiss, 1973).

Academic Counsellor: Academic Counsellor is to help students, develop the necessary skill of learning and study, and confidence in their ability to succeed, which will through the rest of their course.

Learner: A person who is in process of learning in Dr. B. R. Ambedkar Open University to pursue his course in graduation.

Student Support Services (SSS): The philosophy behind Student Support Services (SSS) is to help students to overcome barriers to learning which result from the loneliness of the student working on his own. In a conventional university system such barriers are overcome by the teacher a student rapport in an informal routine. It is felt that strong support service will help in the successful completion of a degree and improve the drop out rate.

Study Centre: The study centre of open university form part of the detached programme of the university framed to provide extensive modern and efficient student support services to its students. The university assigns an important role to contact sessions at these study centres which help students both academically and personally. The study centre is equipped to offer students a range of facilities to help them overcome these problems, through assistance, in addition to providing a common forum for student to interest.

Objectives of the Study

In accordance with the purposes detailed earlier, the objectives of the present investigation have been specified as:

1. To identify the attitude of academic counsellors and learners towards Student Support Services (SSS), provided by Dr. B.R. Ambedkar Open University.
2. To identify their reactions towards:
   (a) Instructional Organization.
   (b) Facilities at Study Centres.
   (c) Assignments.
   (d) Evaluation Procedures.
3. To identify the attitude of academic counsellors in terms of their academic discipline and medium of instruction.
4. To identify the attitude of learners in terms of the following variables i.e., sex, employment status, age, academic discipline and medium of learning.

Delimitation of the Study

The present study is delimited to the academic staff and learners of Dr. B. R. Ambedkar Open University Study Centres of Vijayawada and Guntur only. The study is confined to the sample of learners working towards graduate courses only.

2

Review of Related Literature

This chapter presents the review of studies conducted so far in the field of Distance Education in different university stages. Such an attempt has been made to develop an overall idea about the nature and findings of the previous studies and to arrive at a rationale for the present study. In this context, attempt has been made to classify the studies on the aspects covered by the present study and to analyse their findings in qualitative form. In the process of justifying the need for the present study and the methods adopted therein, the available studies at global level have been referred to. However, while doing the review the studies conducted abroad and in India have been classified separately. The review studies conducted at the world level intends to provide a global outlook on them, the review of Indian studies pin-points the specific issues and concerns of researches on distance education system at the national level.

Organisational aspects: Policies, patterns and growth.

Students: Assessment of needs, their reasons for joining the courses, their background, rate of dropouts, reasons for dropping out of the system/s.

Instructional System: Different components of instruction and evaluation of the instructional processes on the basis of learners perception, their problems and suggestions, their achievement and in-depth analysis of the system.

STUDIES ABROAD

Policies, Patterns and Growth

There have been several attempts in conducting studies on this area. Beardsley (1975), Pawdry (1975), Grimmett (1975), Kinsey (1975), Kuznestov (1975), Meirerhenry (1975), Wedemeyer (1975), Chamberlain (1977), Guiton (1977), Nolan (1977), Perry (1977), Pogano (1977), Sims (1978), Green (1980), Schuyer (1981) and Rumble and Borden (1983) are some of them. The common findings that have been marked in these studies are that the organisation structures are integrated within a larger system of education, usually a larger university complex. Within each education set up, the systems follow certain overall policy statements on their roles and functions. The systems, however, have unique policy making models.

Learners of the System

Needs and Aspirations of Learners

On the areas of needs and aspirations of learner for joining different courses, two types of studies have been conducted. One was at the stage previous to entrance to the courses/before establishment of the institutions and the other was at the post entrance stage.

In the pre-entry stage, in one case of one study in the open university, the UK, the target group learners were asked about their awareness of existence of the open university (Walter Perry, 1977).

The study revealed that over five years (1971–76) in the UK 64 per cent of the total adult population had known about the university. From 1971 to 1976; the percentage of men being aware of the open university, increased from 33 per cent to 76 per cent and the percentage of women increased from 29 per cent to 58 per cent. Further, in the stage of inception of the same institution, a sample survey of 3000 adults revealed that 5 per cent of the total respondents were very much interested in joining the open university courses and 0.9 per cent respondents stated definitely to be amongst first applicants (Perry, 1976). In the case of few correspondence institutions in the UK and Japan the target group learners stated about different reasons for joining the courses, which can be placed under two clusters, such as:

(i) to improve upon academic qualifications, to continue with higher education, use of leisure time and to bring about personal development [Sorgel, 1966, Ministry of Education, Japan, 1975; and Wanieweicz (1981)]; and

(ii) to improve upon occupational efficiency to be placed in higher jobs, to bring about economic efficiency in terms of improvement of living condition (Sorgel, 1966, Wanieweicz, 1981 and McIntosh, 1978).

The studies of second category revealed that the students who had already entered the correspondence education stream had done so because of the above stated reasons (Childs, 1966; National Extension College, 1967; Fairbenks, 1971; Glatter and Wedell, 1971; McIntosh, 1978; Peters, 1978; Idle et. al., 1978). Further, motivation for improvement of social status had prompted many students to join the courses (National Extension College, 1967 and McIntosh, 1978). In one of the studies of second category Wanieweicz, 1981) attempt was made to analyse the motivational factors of students on the basis of age and sex Wanieweicz, 1981). The study revealed that job related goals were the best motivating forces for most of the young men of 18 to 24 years and women of 25 to 44 years. The women of above 45 years age group stated that their joining was motivated by their hobbies, recreation and family concerns. However, it could be observed that factors like: (i) changing personal or family circumstances, and (ii) financial problems for unemployed ones had obstructed the ways of potential students to join the correspondence education programme (McIntosh, 1978).

Characteristics of Learners

Studies concerned with learners' characteristics can be recognised with several background variables like age, sex, marital status, regional background, employment, occupation, social class and academic qualification. Further, in some of the cases, analysis of learners' characteristics were done taking into consideration the courses inside the correspondence education system and the outside parallel systems. With regard to age of the students, it could be found that in the UK very high percentage of correspondence education students belonged to around 30 years of age (Glatter and Wedell, 1971; McIntosh, 1978) in the USA and West Germany around 55 to 56 per cent correspondence students belonged to 35 years age group (Johnstone and Rivera, 1965; Peters, 1965) in Costa Rica very high percentage of students of distance university were below 25 years age group (Rumble and Borden, 1983). In comparison to other adult education course students, the correspondence course students were found to be quite younger (Johnstone and Rivera, 1965).

With regard to the sex of students of correspondence education, the studies conducted in the USA and the UK revealed that most of the students i.e., around 70 per cent were men (Johnstone and Rivera, 1965; Glatter and Wedell, 1971). In the case of Open University, the U.K. the situation of 1971 i.e., 70 per cent men and 30 per cent women, changed towards 56 per cent men and 44 per cent women by the year 1978 (McIntosh, 1978). In Canada, however, the largest percentage of students were women especially from 25 to 34 years age group (Waniewicz, 1981).

Regarding marital status of correspondence students it was found that most of them were married and had children (Meddleton, 1965; Schram, 1967; Short, 1967; Waniewicz, 1981); Glatter and Wedell, 1971; McIntosh, 1978; Rumbh and Borden, 1983.

About residences of students the studies like Peters (1965) and Glatter and Wadell (1971) revealed that in comparison to ruralities more urban based learners were attracted towards correspondence system.

The studies on employment and occupation background of correspondence students revealed that among professional course students, 99 per cent were employed ones whereas in the case of general courses 69 per cent students were having employment (Glatter and Wedell, 1971). It was found in general that employed students were absorbed in several professions as civil servants, industrial workers, library servants, housewives, commerce and private sector oriented professionals, clerical and office staff, administration and management personnel, shop keepers, armed forces personnel etc. (International Correspondence School, 1965, Glatter and Wedell, 1971; McIntosh, 1974).

The academic background of correspondence leaners at university stage was found in varied forms. The open university of UK, which did not insist on formal schooling experiences had attracted one-third of its first batch students during 1971 from non-formal education background and the rest from formal background (McIntosh, 1974). In another study Perry (1976) it could be found that during 1971 only 33 per cent students of the open university were fulfilling the minimum qualification requirements for entry into other British Universities. However, by the year 1975 the students percentage from such category had increased to 46.4. The studies conducted in Minnesota University had revealed that the correspondence students grade points were higher than those of day scholars, evening course students and summer students (Kanun, 1968). However, the studies conducted by Meddleton (1965), Schrams (1967) and Short (1967) revealed different results i.e., the general correspondence students were often less able academically or less qualified than full time students taking similar courses.

Studies on Instructional System of Distance Education

(i) Descriptive Studies

Studies under this category had aimed at description of students participation in instructional programmes, their study habits, problems in studies, etc. In the open university of U. K. (McIntosh, 1974) the majority of students (70 per cent to 80 per cent) choose to watch and listen the instructional programmes broadcast at their leisure. Regarding use of study centres, it was found that in the early weeks many students (50 per cent to 60 per cent) attended them mainly to see counsellors and other students to familiarise themselves with the system. Later on, the attendants percentages receded to 30 per cent or so. As the examination approached, some students were unable to go to study centres. A study conducted by Graham

(1971) on completion of assignments in Mermods revealed that 46 per cent students consulted their friends and family members and 45 per cent consulted available literature, and 18 per cent students left the tasks unresolved. Forty-one per cent students stated that they would have proceeded at the same pace with or without assignments. 21 per cent students expressed that studies would have been completed slowly without assignments, and 37 per cent students commented that assignments caused them complete the course more promptly. Very high percentage (71 per cent) of students called for more comprehensive assignments.

Any study conducted by Idle et. al. (1978) on study pattern of successful external students in Australia revealed that an average students studied about 8 hours per week per subject. There existed much differences due to the varying sizes of the subjects based credit points. Regarding their schedule of study 70 per cent students reported that they follow a set schedule for study. It was found that the city dwellers scheduled their studies better than the country dwellers. Most of the students stated that the textbooks were main sources of information for them. The use of library materials by students depended on the nature of the subject and ready availability of material. Regarding audio cassettes, it could be found that the isolated students used them more often than metropolitan and country students.

(ii) Experimentation on Instructional Processes

A few studies were conducted to study the efficiency of certain methods of instruction over others. Simich (1965) conducted a study of the comparative effectiveness of self instructional methods of learning including PLM and correspondence courses techniques. It was found that the correspondence students out score the individualized instruction group but the difference in achievement scores was not significant. Willingham's (1971) study aimed at studying comparative effectiveness of combination of different groups of methods viz., (1) Students meeting the instructors who used lecture-cum-discussion approaches three times a week; (2) Students meeting tutors once in a week and taking correspondence study; (3) Students taking usual correspondence courses. No significant differences could be marked in the achievement of students who undertook these different methods of instruction. Green (1967) studied the effectiveness of correspondence study methods by using PLM, TV and home works/assignments. The methods were found to be equally effective in comparison to conventional methods of teaching, as there did not exist significant differences between the achievement scores of students undertaking studies through different methods.

Wilson's (1968) experimentation aimed at studying the effect of immediate feedback, planned review of lessons and voice components upon prompt response of assignments by the students and their achievement in examinations. It was found that the students included in the experimental group were somewhat more likely to start, more likely to complete and tried to complete the courses in lesser time. However, there was no additional effect upon the rate of sending assignments and achievement of those students in comparison with students of control group who took usual correspondence courses. Preiffer (1971) studied to determine the effect of letters and postcards of encouragement on rate of submission of assignments. It was found that neither the letters nor the postcards of encouragement resulted in a significant increase in the rate of submission of assignments.

(iii) Reaction of Students towards Instructional System

The reaction studies which included the responses of students entering the course, drop-outs and students completing the courses indicated both positive as well as negative opinions about the instructional process of correspondence education. Regarding efficiency of correspondence studies over regular studies, most of the students expressed a high opinion about the correspondence studies, provided, they included better quality exercises and test materials (Glatter and Wedell, 1971). On this matter most of the students completing the courses successfully commented similarly. However, they pointed out that better correspondence study depended upon regular study of the texts, self-checking exercises followed by assignments and teachers evaluative remarks on them, etc. (Graham, 1971). Most of the students of correspondence courses opined that correspondence studies provided more effective exercise and test materials in comparison part-time oral courses. Also, they were more helpful to assess students progress by themselves (Glatter and Wedell, 1971). While reacting to instructional system most of the dropouts stated that correspondence studies required more work and they lessened their interest in the absence of classroom contact (Sloan, 1966 and Pulley, 1971). However, in Pulley (1971)'s study most of the dropouts stated that the quality of correspondence studies were either superior or equal to other approaches of instruction.

Lockwood (1973) while reacting course evaluation instruments, the evaluations of 87 per cent to 97 per cent of the completers indicate the course:

(a) was equal to or better than comparable residence courses on campus,

(b) met an important need for the participants,

(c) could be learned effectively through correspondence study,

(d) recommended that additional correspondence courses of this type be developed. Nearly 42 per cent said they would take another correspondence while 15 per cent said they would not.

Woolsey, Paul Warren (1974) on Evaluation of Correspondence Education found:

(a) Correspondence education is an effective method for individuals who possess the personal characteristics necessary for successful completion of correspondence course.

(b) Correspondence graduates can compete successfully for jobs in their area of study.

(c) Alternatives to the present evaluation procedures do exist, and include accreditation by the National Home Study Council and evaluation by an agency such as CASE.

(d) Present procedures used to qualify to sit for such examinations test for individuals background rather than his job, knowledge and skills.

Robert Mike (1978) in his study on open systems approach to professional education, revealed an adequately designed model, a high degree of openness, a performance oriented curriculum and student support systems, as well as an objective based instructional system.

Carpenter (1981) attempted to study the significant difference between completers and non-completers of correspondence courses in self actualizing levels.

(a) It was concluded that completion of correspondence courses did not provide a good indicator of self-direction in learning for the population utilized in this study, some of which could not be adequately met through completion of highly structured correspondence courses. Therefore, no conclusions concerning the relationship of self-direction in learning and self-actualization could be drawn from this study.

(b) The findings suggested that the needs of adult learners who enroll in university correspondence study for non-credit reasons are not being fully met under the present structure of rigid requirements and limited course content.

STUDIES IN INDIA

Studies on Policies and Patterns of Distance Education

Studies of above category covers enquiries regarding policies concerning distance education systems, nature of courses and level of courses offered through distance education, enrolment, physical facilities etc., in the Indian context. The first study of this category was conducted by Dutt (1976). The study was conducted on the trend of enrolment in correspondence courses from 1971 to 1976 taking into consideration the nature of courses, annual compound rate of enrolment and levels of courses. There have been instances of studies on organization aspects of correspondence courses by Singh (1976), Anand (1979), Biswal (1979), Rao (1980), Khan (1982), Nagaraju (1982), Dutt (1984), Pugazentus (1985), Sahoo (1985), Balasubrahmaniam (1986), Sudama and Pugazenthi (1986); U.G.C. (1986), Dutt (1989), Sahoo (1989), and Satpathy (1989). Almost all the studies highlighted on gradual growth of distance education in the country which were of traditional type. There has been mere extension of the system of regular courses offered through traditional universities. Therefore, the courses had limitations in meeting academic and socio-economic needs of learners of distance education system. Biswal (1979)'s study, which had covered almost all the correspondence institutions of India revealed that

(a) the objectives of correspondence courses offered through different universities remained similar all over the country;

(b) the academic staff pattern remained more or less similar in all the universities, whereas differences were witnessed with regard to administrative staff pattern;

(c) enrolment rate was found to be higher in Arts, Commerce, and Education disciplines in comparison to others.

Besides, UGC (1986) study revealed that the enrolment of distance education institutions in India has varied from 500 (Meerut) to 68,554 (Madhurai). There was tremendous imbalance amongst regions with regard to enrolment. Dutt (1986) reported that distance education institutions in southern region enrolled 9.5 per cent students of total enrolment in universities and colleges of concerned region, whereas eastern region has only 0.4 per cent representation of total enrolment in distance education institutions. At State level Himachal Pradesh and Tamilnadu have enrolled 42 per cent and 22 per cent of students of respective State level total enrolment in higher education. Sahoo (1989) found a similar trend of enrolment in distance education during 1986–87. In spite of high level enrolment in distance education there were 11 universities out of 26 during 1982 which were treated as non-viable units because of admitting less than 2500 students.

It was revealed by UGC (1986) that the institutes of correspondence courses were treated as separate unit of universities. However, they are governed by the rules which are usually framed for regular courses and found inappropriate for distance education. As the status of distance education institutions inside traditional structure was neither of a teaching department nor that of a college, powers and status of Directors remained undefined.

Satpathy's (1989) study highlighted on future expansion

of distance education system in terms of national and state level open university system, innovative practices in means and media of distance education system, and growth of enrolment up to almost 25 per cent of total enrolment of higher education by 2001 in the country. This has been visualized that changes would occur in organization of distance education functioning inside traditional university system. Sahoo's (1989) analysis of enrolment of distance education including correspondence courses and open universities revealed that towards 21st century (by 2002 AD) the enrolment position of distance education would reach at 10.21 lakhs, provided, trend of past 25 years is followed in a linear form.

Studies on Learners of Distance Education

A large number of studies conducted in India have focussed on study of learners of distance education system. Some of these studies emphasise on needs and aspirations of learners motivation to continue with courses till its completion, and factors influencing learners of decisions to pursue their studies. Most of the studies conducted on learners, have concentrated on socio-psychological characteristics of learners who continue with distance education. Moreover, a few studies have been conducted on those learners who have discontinued the courses before its completion.

Needs, Motivations and Aspirations of Learners

Studies of Anand (1979), Khan (1982), Koul (1982), Kumar et. al. (1982), Pillai and Mohan (1983), Singh (1983), Sahoo (1985), UGC (1986), and Misra (1988) revealed that improvement of qualification and desire for continuing with higher education acted as major motivation for joining correspondence courses. Kumar et. al. (1982), Pillai and Mohan (1983), Sahoo (1985), and Misra (1988) identified other motivators like improvement in own profession and getting chances for further promotion in own field. Moreover some sociological factors like improvement of social status of learners have been identified as motivators of distance education learners [Pillai and Mohan (1983); Sahoo (1985); and UGC (1986)].

A comparative study (Biswal), 1979 on academic motivation of students of distance education and regular courses revealed that correspondence courses students had lower level academic motivation than that of their regular course counterparts. At the university stage, the students joined correspondence courses in preference to regular courses or appearing in the examinations privately because of several personal and socio-economic reasons. The reasons as identified by Kohl (1982) and Sahoo (1985), were non-availability of time, mental maturity of learners, non-existence of college in locality and heavy expenses in formal college education. Several background factors like age, employment, paucity of time, poor financial condition in last qualifying examination had major links with these reasons (Khan, 1982 and Sahoo, 1985). At secondary stage, Singh (1980) and (1983) found that learners preferred correspondence courses to regular schooling because of employment status of learners; involvement in household activities, non-availability of facility for schooling, and failures/or dropping out of regular courses.

Studies conducted on university level students (Sahoo, 1985, UGC, 1986) revealed that very large number of correspondence students decided to join the courses on their own. Sahoo (1985) identified homogeneity in the responses of learners at entrance stage, students at the course completion stage and those who passed courses with regard to their expectations from correspondence courses. Kohl (1982) found that in the case of dropouts of distance education the reasons for joining their courses were of academic and personal type. As in the case of students who continue with studies the dropouts of distance education had joined the distance education because of their curiosity of learning new discipline, to obtain professional training and to obtain additional qualification.

Studies on Background of Distance Education Students

Studies on distance education students' socio-economic and academic backgrounds reveal meaningful facts regarding distance education system in the country. Unlike the age cohart of regular college students of 16 to 23 the age majority of students of correspondence students belonged to the age group of 16 to 35 years (Anand, 1979; Gomathi, 1982; Khan, 1982; Pillai and Mohan, 1983; Sahoo, 1985, and UGC, 1986), while of most of the lower age (16–25) group students continued with undergraduate courses (Khan, 1982; Sahoo, 1985 and UGC, 1986) most of the upper age students (20–60) continued with post-graduate courses (Sahoo, 1985). In the case of one of the diploma of programme Indira Gandhi National Open University large chunk of students belonged to 30 to 40 years age group (Misra, 1988). The majority of learners population were men (Biswal, 1979; Gomathi, 1982; Pillai and Mohan, 1983) and Sahoo, 1985; employed background and belonged to different cadres of vocations like teaching, clericals, administrative, sales workers, service workers, farmers, mechanics and labourers with major concentration on teaching and clerical jobs (Gomathi, 1982; Pillai and Mohan, 1983; Sahoo, 1985 and UGC, 1986). Almost all the students of management course of IGNOU were employed ones and a large chunk of them had less than 10 years service experience. However, students with more than 25 years were admitted into the course (Misra, 1988). A sizeable number of them (30 per cent) were first generation learners. Moreover, a large number of learners had 1 to 10 years gap between their last qualifying examination and enrolment in present courses (Sahoo, 1985). With regard to socio-psychological characteristics of school level students of correspondence courses Singh (1980), (1983) found that the age range of students varied from below 20 to 40 years range with major (Deval, 1982). Majority of students belonged to men group, married group, upper castes and moderate economic positions. Around one-third students of distance education at school level were having employed status (Singh, 1980, 1983; and Deval, 1982).

Studies on Dropouts

Discontinuation of studies has been a general feature of distance education system.

Major problems coming on the ways of dropouts were: Lack of availability of time to pursue studies, non-attendance of contact programmes, lack of proper teacher students interactions; non-availability of reference materials; not submitting required number of assignments and difficulties in studying the lesson scripts (Konl, 1982, and Sahoo, 1985).

The dropouts needed improvements in managerial,. instructional and evaluation system of distance education (Konl, 1982 and Sahoo, 1985).

Studies on Teachers and Supportive Staff in Distance Education

Studies conducted on traditional system of distance education revealed that instructional and evaluation activities are carried out by internal faculty members as well as outside institution teachers. The major share of instructional activities especially the production of print material and teaching during personal contact programmes were performed by outside teachers. Quite a large number of teachers involved in distance education institutions were found to be lesser experienced in teaching and research work (Sahoo, 1985). None of the teachers were formally trained in performing instructional activities of distance education. Most of the internal faculty members of distance education institutions had expressed willingness to undergo such training courses (Khan, 1982; Sahoo, 1985, and Konl, 1988). While teaching faculty of correspondence courses were supposed to have some minimum requirements as needed for teachers of university teaching departments, the teachers of correspondence courses did not get equal status at par with university teachers to most of the universities.

Instructional Processes of Distance Education

Researches on these aspects in India emphasise on studying effectiveness of different methods and media in experimental situations studying the existing processes of instructional and evaluation programmes in distance education institutions, studying the usefulness of different components of instructional activities and evaluation system and participants' reaction about the functioning of instructional system has been identified. Major instructional activities of distance education have been restricted to print based materials and occasional interaction between tutor and students through assignments and personal contact programmes. Instructional activities also have been carried out through electronic media like radio, TV, audio cassettes, video cassettes and computer programmes (Anand, 1979; Biswal, 1979; Khan, 1982; Pillai and Mohan, 1982;

Sahoo, 1985, Balasubrahmanian, 1986, Kumar and Mohan, 1982).

The studies conducted on different aspects of instruction can be stated as follows.

Print Based Material

This has been witnessed that all of the distance education institutions at university level as well as school level give major emphasis on print based instructional material. The materials may be of modular forms of self-instructional programmed learning packages and some other types as per certain formats as prescribed by respective institutions (Biswal, 1979; Singh, 1980; Khan, 1982; Singh, 1983; Sahoo, 1985). This was found that a large majority of students of university level courses (81 to 85 per cent) depend on print based scripts for completing their studies (Anand, 1979; Khan, 1982; Sahoo, 1985).

All the studies reported about the usefulness of lesson scripts as perceived by the students in one or the other respect (And, 1979; Biswal, 1979; Singh, 1980; Khan, 1982; Pillai and Mohan, 1982; Sahoo, 1985; Kumar, 1985; UGC, 1986). In most of the cases, the lesson scripts of respective distance education institutions did not follow systematic format of lesson preparation. While most of students, dropouts and products of distance education expressed moderate views about different aspects of lessons like style of presentation, content clarity, suggested references and languages (Sahoo, 1985) majority of students and dropout reacted about their difficulties in study of lesson scripts (Singh, 1980; and 1983; Deval, 1982, Koul, 1982; Khan, 1982; Sahoo, 1985). A large number of students (41 per cent) of six universities found crowded schedules in the lessons and faced difficulties in studying all the lessons. Moreover irregular despatch system of lessons created problems for students (Singh, 1980; Nagaraju, 1982; Koul, 1982, Singh, 1983; Sahoo, 1985).

Assignment System

Assignment system is treated as one of the key components of student support services in distance education. Assignment system was found useful by most of the students of universities like H.P. University (Biswal, 1979; Regional Colleges of Education, Kumar, 1986).

Most of the students appreciated compulsory submission of assignments since most of the students who received evaluated response sheets in time bound assignment system useful to some extent (Sahoo, 1985). Distance Education Institutions did not make serious efforts to clarify students doubts (Deval, 1982; Nagaraju, 1982; Sahoo, 1985).

Personal Contact Programme (PCPs)

All the institutions of Distance Education had the provision for personal contact programmes (Dutt, 1976 and Biswal, 1979).

Compulsion, optional provision of attendance, selection of venue of PCPs, employment positions of learners, lack of proper facilities for boarding and lodging, lack of prior information to students acted as influential factors in students attendance in PCPs (Sahoo, 1985).

Sahoo (1985) found that in the case of compulsory provision of attendance 70 to 80 per cent students turned up for PCPs, whereas in the case of voluntary attendance around 33 per cent students attended the PCPs of PG courses. The usual methods used for teaching in the PCPs were lecture, and question answers (Sahoo, 1985). The utilities of attendance was experienced by students in terms of clarification of doubts, getting inspirations for further studies, better preparation for examination and solving academic problems (Mathur, 1979; Sahoo, 1985; Balasubramaniam, 1985). The students have appreciated teacher students informal interactions during PCPs (Sahoo, 1985). Most of the respondents among teachers, students and dropouts had expressed opinions for increasing the frequencies of PCPs (Sahoo, 1985) and increasing the duration of each PCP (Bhusan and Sharma, 1976; Anand, 1979; and Sahoo, 1985).

The common suggestion in above studies regarding PCPs were that proper care must be taken for selection of venues, sending prompt information to participants, division of students into appropriate groups and to organize discussions would provide variety and utility.

Different aspects of distance education were studied scientifically both in India and abroad. Also there are some studies relating to SSS. But evidently there is not much of research activity relating to SSS in the study centres of Ambedkar Open University in Guntur and Vijayawada cities. Hence the present study.

3
Method of Investigation

Dr. B.R. Ambedkar Open University based on the concept of 'Open Learning', the University represents a unique system of realizing the democratization of higher education and the ideal of continuing education. It's instruction was through multimedia approach. So its success depends mainly on instructional organization or methods that are in use. Dr. B. R. Ambedkar Open University keeping in view the characteristics of Distance Education learners, it was planned Student Support Services (SSS) in order to clarify their academic problems. If SSS are not maintained well, the students may face problems to continue with their studies.

For effective reach out of these SSS, Academic Counsellors play an important role through study centres for the benefit of the students.

The present study is an attempt made to find out the attitudes on Academic Counsellors and Learners towards the Student Support Services of Dr. B.R. Ambedkar Open University. Dr. B. R. Ambedkar Open University providing SSS to learners through study centres in different centres with certain facilities viz., print medium, academic counselling, audio-visual facilities and Personal Contact Programme (PCP).

It is necessary to find out how far the SSS are effectively organized for the benefit of the learners. There is a real need for objective and systematic study of SSS of Open University through Study Centres. The results of such studies will provide the administrators scientifically obtained information. It will help them to know the weak and strong points of the SSS. The result will facilitate them to take correct decisions to formulate or revise policies and to modify the actual operations of the SSSs.

The Academic Counsellors are the backbone for effective use of all planned plans in the form of Student Support Services and the success depends largely on the ability of these academic counsellors.

Learners in Open University take admissions with different aspirations. Here the characteristics of learners also differ in age, in job, some are to refresh their knowledge in their own fields, some are to improve their qualification for promotion. So they are highly self-motivated and matured in all aspects. Learners are the real consumers of SSS of Open University.

Hence there is every need to identify the attitudes of Academic Counsellors and Learners with regard to the organization and functioning of SSSs.

Taking into account above circumstances, caused for inspiration for undertaking this study came from limited studies of this type conducted abroad and from realization of its importance and possibilities of its practical utility in Indian set up.

The objectives, the procedure of the study and the tools used are described below:

The objectives of the study are:

1. To identify the attitude of academic counsellors and learners towards student support services (SSS), provided by Dr. B.R. Ambedkar Open University.

2. To identify their reactions towards:

   (a) Instructional organization.

   (b) Facilities at study centres.

   (c) Assignments.

   (d) Evaluation procedures.

3. To identify the attitude of academic counsellors in terms of their academic discipline and medium of instruction.
4. To identify the attitude of learners in terms of the following variables namely sex, employment status, age, academic discipline and medium of learning.

Types of Researches

Educational research can be considered as an accumulation of knowledge in the form of concepts and facts organized in relation to generalization of purposes. It can also be considered as a method of establishing general proposals by techniques of observation, classification and deductive process.

There are many ways and means of gathering, analysing and reporting research data. Educationists are not in the thorough agreement as to the so-called method of collecting and handling the data. Research studies are distinguished on the basis of their purposes and approaches and this may technically be called difference in methods. But these methods do not significantly differ in their procedure, selection, formulation and definition of the problem. Survey of related information, collection, analysis and interpretation of new data and reporting of the work done are the steps common to all types of research methods. Three important methods of investigation are generally followed in the field of educational research. John Best (1983) classified Educational Research into the following three types:

(i) Historical.

(ii) Normative of Descriptive or Survey Research.

(iii) Experimental Research.

Historical Research: Historical Research approach is of universal application in the studies of the social field. This method is considered with the past and attempts to trace the past as a measure of seeing the past in perspective. It helps the property evaluated past in the light of these standard sound conditions of life then prevailing and arriving at general solutions that are helpful in knowing the present and predicting the future.

Normative or Survey or Descriptive Research: Normative Research deals with "what is" and "what exist". It describes and interprets what exists at present. According to John Best (1983) descriptive research is concerned with conditions or attitudes that exists, practices that prevail beliefs, points or view or attitudes that are held processes that are followed, differences that are held or trends that are developed. Writers have used various teams like normative, descriptive, survey status or trend to describe such type of investigation. John Best (1983) has preferred to use the term "Descriptive Research". This method of gathering data from a relatively large number of cases at a particular time. This method is cross sectional in nature and considered with the characteristics of individuals. It involves definite objectives and clearly defined problems. It requires expert and imaginative planning, careful analysis and interpretations.

The investigator adopted this method for the present investigation.

Experimental Research: Experimental Research describes "what will be" when certain factors are carefully controlled. It is the classical methodology of the science laboratory and is probably the most difficult and most exacting of all methods of research. While "experimental research" finds its greatest utility and application in the laboratory, where conditions can be rigorously controlled, it has been applied with success in the classroom where within certain limitations, significant factors or conditions can be controlled.

The present study falls under descriptive or survey method of research. The tools that are generally followed in research are described briefly below:

To carry out any of the types of research study, data are gathered from which hypothesis may be tested. A great variety of research tools have been developed to help in gathering data. These tools are many kinds and employ distinctive ways of describing and qualifying the data. Each tool is particularly appropriate for the certain sources of data yielding information of the kind and in the form that would be most effectively used.

The major tools of research in education can be classified broadly into the following categories:

(A) Inquiry Forms.

1. Questionnaire.
2. Schedule.
3. Check-list.
4. Rating Scale.
5. Opinionnaire or attitude scale.

(B) Observation.

(C) Interview.

(D) Sociometry.

Psychological tests:

1. Achievement test.
2. Attitude test.
3. Intelligence test.
4. Interest Inventory.
5. Personality Means.

The research worker may use one or more of the tools in combination. Barr Davis and Johnson (1952) define questionnaire as "A systematic compilation of questions that are submitted to a sampling of population from which information is desired."

Questionnaire falls under data gathering devices which make use of properly prepared forms for inquiring into and securing information about certain phenomena under study. Generally the word 'questionnaire' refers to a device for securing answers to questions by using a form which the respondent fills in himself.

The questionnaire has an important place in educational research. It is a simple and clear form to get objective results in the best possible way. The present study has been undertaken by adopting the questionnaire method.

The questionnaire was developed and used for collecting the opinions of the persons included in the sample for investigation. The study aimed at knowing the degree of acceptance or divergence from one's opinion to the other among the individuals in the sample.

After going through various previous investigations and research papers published on the subject, the researcher constructed an attitude scale consisting of four areas related to SSS. The preliminary tool consisted of 62 items. For identifying the attitude Likert Scaling was adopted and the sample was asked to respond on three point scale.

Description of the Tool

The tool aimed at measuring attitude of academic counsellors and learners towards SSS of Dr. B. R. Ambedkar Open University on the following areas namely:

1. Regarding instructional organization of Open University.
2. Regarding the facilities at Study Centres.
3. Assignments.
4. Evaluation procedures followed at Open University.

Now the area-wise description is presented below :

Area I: Regarding Instructional Organization of Open University

In this section the academic counsellors were asked to express their opinions about their academic involvement, courses and their syllabi of their own subjects, preparation of course materials, usefulness and also reach of the course materials to students at three degree courses namely, B.A., B.Com., and B.Sc.

The same items were used to know of the opinions of learners also.

Area II: Study Centres of Open University

In this section, the teachers were asked to give their opinion on the following aspects of the study centres:

Physical facilities in the Study Centres namely rooms for contact session, academic counselling facilities by part-time counsellors, audio-visual equipment facilities and library facilities.

Organization of teaching activities and guidance provided to the students through personal contact programme. And to know the extent to which PCPs are helpful to solve their academic problems and to develop rapport between teachers and students.

Area III: Assignments

This area also for both teachers and students.

This aspect dealt with the items meant to study the reactions of assignment evaluators to the present system of evaluation of assignments. Also the teachers were asked about the problems they faced in connection with evaluation of assignments and suggestions for solution of those problems. It is also about students problems in writing their assignments.

Area IV: Evaluation Procedures followed at Open University

In this section, the teachers and students were asked to express their opinions to the present practices of evaluation of students performances. The aspects covered under this section were about the nature of assignments, coverage of assignments, regularity in evaluation of assignments, the place of assignments in consideration to the award of degrees, nature of questions asked in the annual examinations and the introduction of new system of evaluation. The teachers were also asked to state about their difficulties with regard to their role as evaluators considering the above aspects.

The students were also asked to express their opinions.

Variables

The main variables of the study is academic counsellors verses learners. Further analysis is also attempted in terms of the following instructor related and learner related variables.

Academic Counsellor Variables

1. Subject handled—Arts/Commerce/Science—B.A.; B.Com., and B.Sc.
2. Medium of Instruction: English/Telugu.

Learner Variables

1. Sex.
2. Employed/unemployed.
3. Faculty-wise : B.A., B.Com., and B.Sc.
4. Age.
5. Medium of Learning—English/Telugu.

Pilot Study

In order to finalise the statements in the attitude scale, the pilot study was conducted on the sample of 50 comprising of 15 academic counsellors and 35 learners. For this total sample chi-square values for items in the attitude scale were calculated and interpreted at .05 level.

Since three point scale was adopted according to Table 'E' in Garrett:

f = 2 and P at .05 level is 5.991.

Those items with a chi-square value of 5.991 were deleted from the final tool.

The chi-square values and the numbers of items not included in the final form of the tool are given in the Table 3.1.

Table 3.1: Chi-square Values for All the Items

N=50

Item No.	*2 Value*	*Item No.*	*2 Value*	*Item No.*	*2 Value*
1.	25.4	22.	23.6	43.	12.2
2.	20.2	23.	13.4	44.	11.9
3.	13.4	24.	4.9*	45.	19.4
4.	15.9	25.	15.4	46.	24.6
5.	16.2	26.	5.6*	47.	20.2
6.	11.9	27.	5.1*	48.	12.4
7.	12.0	28.	4.9*	49.	13.9
8.	22.4	29.	16.4	50.	12.4
9.	24.2	30.	12.4	51.	4.8*
10.	11.9	31.	12.2	52.	5.3*
11.	21.2	32.	13.4	53.	18.3
12.	21.2	33.	12.4	54.	5.4*
13.	12.4	34.	19.6	55.	25.3
14.	5.8*	35.	20.2	56.	5.2*
15.	26.4	36.	13.4	57.	20.4
16.	15.6	37.	12.2	58.	4.8*
17.	5.6*	38.	30.4	59.	11.2
18.	16.4	39.	28.6	60.	22.4
19.	22.6	40.	5.8*	61.	18.2
20.	21.4	41.	12.4	62.	20.4
21.	15.2	42.	24.6		

* Not included in final form of the tool.

Tool

The following is the attitude scale consisting of 50 items.

Area I : Regarding Instructional Organization of Open University

1. Involvement of Personnel is according to their abilities — A U D

2.	Students are satisfied with the academic activity.	A	U	D
3.	Student needs are properly considered in the courses offered at Open University.	A	U	D
4.	The course material prepared by Open University is adequate.	A	U	D
5.	Course materials are good.	A	U	D
6.	The course materials currently in use need no revision.	A	U	D
7.	Illustrations in the course materials are satisfactory.	A	U	D
8.	Course materials supplied to learners are useful.	A	U	D
9.	Students can put to use the course materials.	A	U	D
10.	Course materials reach the learners in time.	A	U	D
11.	Course material supplied is suitable to the level of learners.	A	U	D

Area II : Study Centres of Open University

12.	The facilities at study centres are accessible to all.	A	U	D
13.	They have good library facilities.	A	U	D
14.	They have good audio-visual facilities.	A	U	D
15.	The number of instructional days are sufficient.	A	U	D
16.	Counselling days are sufficient.	A	U	D
17.	Counselling days are convenient.	A	U	D
18.	The timings are suitable to learners.	A	U	D
19.	The quality of counselling is satisfactory.	A	U	D

20. Counselling helps students. A U D
21. Counsellor is helping the students to solve their academic problem. A U D
22. Physical facilities are satisfactory. A U D
23. P.C.P. is useful to students. A U D
24. Teachers services during PCP are satisfactory. A U D
25. Most teachers do not find it difficult to clarify the doubts of students. A U D
26. The teacher student rapport during PCP is satisfactory. A U D
27. The PCP can initiate the learners towards proper learning. A U D
28. It helps students in improving their learning skills. A U D
29. It helps students to improve their study habits. A U D
30. Suitability of PCP timings to students is important. A U D
31. PCP venues are accessible to learners. A U D

Area III : Assignments

32. Students submit them regularly. A U D
33. The assignments are useful to learners. A U D
34. The learner feels the importance of the assignments. A U D
35. Assignments completion is time consuming. A U D
36. Sufficient number of assignments are given. A U D
37. They are given in terms of instructional goals. A U D

38. They help the students to develop proper learning habits. A U D
39. The assignments can help the students in developing proper study skills. A U D
40. The assignments help students to evaluate themselves. A U D
41. The academic counsellors are not over burdened with assignment work. A U D
42. They are trained in proper evaluation of student assignments. A U D

Area IV : Evaluation at Open University

43. The evaluation procedures are satisfactory. A U D
44. They are useful. A U D
45. Evaluation procedures are uniform. A U D
46. Evaluation at Open University means passing the university examination only. A U D
47. It is comprehensive. A U D
48. Getting good assignemnt grades is as important as passing final examination. A U D
49. Comprehensive evaluation may be taken into consideration for awarding degrees to students. A U D
50. Evaluation of assignments is not a time consuming process. A U D

Validity and Reliability of the Tool

Since sufficient importance was given to each area in constructing the attitude scale, it was considered that content validity of the tool is established. The reliability of the tool was calculated after its final administration. Split half method was used for calculating the reliability.

The reliability of the tool by split half method is 0.84

Administration of the Tool

Three hundred questionnaires got prepared for the purpose of this study. Much care was taken to get the questionnaire printed correctly and neatly. Then they were personally handed over to the academic counsellors and learners. Due regard was given for subject-wise and medium of instruction-wise as variables.

Altogether 100 questionnaires each for academic counsellors at two centres were given.

The final questionnaire was given to a sample of 100 learners of Vijayawada study centre located at Siddhartha Arts College and to another 100 students of Hindu College, Guntur Centre.

The questionnaire was administered personally at the study centres on academic counsellors and learners. The sample of academic counsellors who returned questionnaires were 54 from both the centres and of learners was 102.

Altogether the percentage of questionnaires returned from the sample was fifty.

The following table shows variable distribution of the sample.

Table 3.2: Variable Distribution of Sample

Category			Sample-wise
1. Academic Counsellors		...	54
Learners		...	102
2. Academic Counsellor Variables :			
(a) Academic discipline :	Arts		23
	Commerce		14
	Science		17
(b) Medium of Instruction :	English		14
	Telugu		36
3. Learner Variables :			
(a) Sex :	Men	...	49
	Women	...	53
(b) Employment Status :	Employed		38
	Unemployed		64

Table 3.2: Contd..

Category			*Sample-wise*
(c) Age :	Below 25	...	19
	Between 26 - 45	...	75
	Above 45	...	8
(d) Academic Discipline :	Arts		57
	Commerce		38
	Science		17
(e) Medium of Learning :	English		18
	Telugu		84

Sample

The sample for this investigation consisted of 54 academic counsellors of the study centres of Vijayawada and Guntur.

The learner sample for this investigation was 102 from both the centres.

In both the centres the population of learners was around 2000. The questionnaire was administered to random sample of learner totalling 102 i.e., 5 per cent of the population was contacted by random sampling.

Similarly the population of academic counsellor is around 120 and 54 academic counsellors were contacted i.e., around 45 per cent of the academic counsellors.

The Scoring Procedure

The questionnaire was administered on a three point scale showing agreement, undecided and disagreement with each statement. For identifying the attitude of the sample weighted score technique was adopted and item mean scores were computed.

Weightages given are agreement 3 points, undecided 2 points and disagreement 1 point.

The formula for item mean score is :

$$\text{Item Mean Score} = \frac{\text{Weightage Score}}{\text{N}}$$

Item mean score of less than 2 denotes tendency towards disagreement.

Item mean score of 2.5 and above positive agreement in the statement.

Item mean score of 1.5 and less positive disagreement with the statement, description of sample and data are given in the coming chapter.

For each individual an over all attitude score was also calculated. Since number of attitude items in the scale were 50. The highest attitude score possible is 150 and least score is 50.

Since mid-point falls at 100, any score above 100 denotes a tendency towards positive attitude. Similarly scores less than 100 denote a tendency towards negative attitude.

Attitude scores are interpreted according to the following scale.

Attitude score of 126 above	...	Positive attitude.
Between 125 and 100	...	Just positive.
Between 100 and 75	...	Just negative.
Less than 74	...	Negative.

For each of the samples mean attitude score were calculated and compared for significance at 0.05 level.

Wherever the difference was significant, item mean scores were calculated and the differences of opinion analysed.

4
Data, Conclusions and Suggestions

Student Support Services (SSS) play an important role in the process of Distance Education. This study of the attitude of counsellors and learners attempts to identify the nature of attitude held by them towards SSS.

The data was statistically analysed and presented in the following pages.

Attitude of academic counsellors and learners towards SSS.

Table 4.1 shows a comparison of the mean attitude scores of counsellors and learners.

Table 4.1: Comparison of the Mean Attitude Scores of Counsellors and Learners

	N	*Mean*	*S.D.*	*M.D.*	*S.E$_d$.*	*C.R.*
Counsellors	54	128.3	11.23	5.7	1.96	2.91*
Learners	102	122.6	12.36			

* Significant at 0.05 level.

As can be seen from the Table 4.1 the C. R. value is significant at .05 level.

Hence it is concluded that there is a difference in the attitude of counsellors and learners towards SSS.

The academic counsellors hold a more positive attitude than learners.

Table 4.2 shows the distribution of attitude scores in the samples.

Table 4.2: Distribution of Attitude Scores in the Samples

Score Average	*Attitude Description*	*Counsellors N %*	*Learners N %*
125 and above	Positive	40%	50%
125 – 100	Just Positive	12%	40%
100 – 75	Just Negative	2%	12%
Less than 75	Negative	---	---

As can be seen from the Table 4.2 more than 40 per cent of the counsellors hold positive attitude towards SSS while only 50 per cent of the learners hold positive attitude. It is also significant to note that 12 per cent of the learners have a tendency towards negative attitude.

Table 4.3 shows a comparison of item mean scores for counsellors and learners.

An item mean score of 2.5 and above is considered as agreement with the statement and item mean score of less than 2.5 as disagreement.

Table 4.3: Item Mean Scores Comparison (Counsellors Versus Learners)

Item No.	*Counsellors*	*Learners*	*Item No.*	*Counsellors*	*Learners*
1.	2.6	2.5	6.	2.1 D	2.1 D
2.	2.5	2.5	7.	2.5	2.5
3.	2.6	2.2 D*	8.	2.7	2.6
4.	2.6	2.5	9.	2.5	2.6
5.	1.8 D	1.9 D	10.	1.5 D	1.3 D

Contd.

Table 4.3 : (Contd.)

Item No.	*Counsellors*	*Learners*	*Item No.*	*Counsellors*	*Learners*
11.	2.6	1.8 D*	31.	2.5	2.6
12.	2.6	1.7 D*	32.	1.8 D	2.5*
13.	2.6	1.8 D*	33.	2.5	2.6
14.	2.6	2.5	34.	1.9 D	2.5*
15.	2.6	2.7	35.	1.9 D	1.8 D
16.	1.8 D	1.9 D	36.	2.5	2.6
17.	2.5	2.5	37.	2.6	2.5
18.	2.6	2.7	38.	2.5	2.5
19.	2.6	2.5	39.	2.6	2.5
20.	2.7	2.6	40.	2.5	1.9 D*
21.	2.7	2.7	41.	2.5	2.6
22.	2.6	2.6	42.	1.6 D	2.5*
23.	2.7	2.7	43.	2.5	2.5
24.	2.6	2.5	44.	2.6	2.6
25.	2.6	2.6	45.	2.5	2.5
26.	2.6	2.5	46.	1.6 D	1.7 D
27.	2.8	2.6	47.	2.5	2.5
28.	2.7	2.7	48.	2.5	2.6
29.	2.6	2.5	49.	2.6	2.6
30.	2.5	2.6	50.	2.5	2.5

D – Disagreement with the statement.
* – Difference of opinion.
No Mark – Agreement with the statement.

As can be seen from the Table 4.3 of the 50 statements, the counsellors have agreed with 41 statements and disagreed with 9 statements.

The learners have agreed with 39 statements and disagreed with 11 statements.

A comparison of the item mean scores of counsellors and learners shows that there is a difference of opinion on seven statements.

A comparative description of above aspects is given below in an area-wise manner.

Area I: Instructional Organization

The counsellors and learners are of the opinion that the involved personnel are according to their abilities. The learners are satisfied with academic activity.

They further felt that the course material prepared by Open University is adequate and illustrations in course material are satisfactory.

Both counsellors are learners are of the opinion that course material supplied to learners are useful and the course material is found usable.

However, they expressed the feeling that the course material currently in use needs revision.

They also unanimously opined that the course material do not reach the learners in time.

However they expressed different opinions on two statements.

While counsellors felt that the students needs are properly considered in the courses offered at Open University, the learners felt otherwise.

While the counsellors were satisfied that the course material supplied is to the level of learners, the learners felt that it is not suitable.

Area II: Facilities at Study Centres

In this area the sample was asked to reach to statements about facilities and personal contact programme (PCP) at study centres.

In this area the counsellors have agreed with 19 statements and disagreed with one statement. The learners disagreed with three statements and agreed with seventeen statements.

There was difference of opinion on two statements.

Both the counsellors and learners feel that the study centres have good audio-visual facilities.

They have expressed satisfaction that the instructional days are sufficient. However, both felt that the counselling days are not sufficient. They admitted that counselling days are convenient and the times are suitable to learners. They feel that the quality of counselling is satisfactory and that counselling helps students. They admitted that the counsellor is helping the students to solve their academic problems.

Regarding physical facilities during PCP, both the samples expressed the opinion that they are satisfactory. They further felt that PCP is useful to students.

They are of the opinion that teachers services during PCP are satisfactory and most teachers do not find it difficult to clarify the doubts of the students. They are of the opinion that the teacher student rapport during PCP is satisfactory. Both the samples of counsellors and learners felt that PCP initiates the learners towards proper learning. They felt that it helps students in improving their learning skills and to improve their study habits. They feel that PCP venues are accessible to learners and the timings suitable.

While counsellors feel the facilities at study centres are accessible to all, the learners have disagreed with them. The learners have further expressed dissatisfaction about library facilities. Probably it is because of non-availability of books in the medium in which majority are studying.

Area III: Assignments

In this area about assignments the counsellors have agreed with seven statements and disagreed with four statements. The learners have disagreed with two statements and agreed with nine statements. There was difference of opinion on three statements.

The counsellors and learners felt that the assignments are useful to students. They further admitted that sufficient number of assignments are given and they are given in terms of instructional goals. Both the samples felt that the assignments help the students to develop proper learning habits and study skills. They felt that the academic counsellors are not over burdened with assignment valuation work.

They are of the opinion that assignment completion is not time consuming. However, the counsellors feel that the learners do not feel the importance of assignment whereas the learners disagree with them. The learners feel that the assignments do not help them to evaluate themselves.

The counsellors expressed the need for training in proper evaluation of students' assignments.

Area IV: Evaluation Procedures

In this area both counsellors and learners have expressed the same trend of opinions. They agreed with seven statements and disagreed with one statement.

Both the samples feel that the evaluation procedure are satisfactory. They are found useful and uniform. Further they are of the opinion that the evaluation is comprehensive and getting good assignment grades is as important as passing final examination.

They are of the opinion that evaluation of assignments is not time consuming process. They felt that comprehensive evaluation may be taken into consideration for awarding degrees to students.

Analysis of Variables

As already described for each sub-sample scores, mean and standard deviations are calculated. Variable-wise comparisons were made to identify the influencing variables.

As can be seen from the Table 4.4 the C. R. values are not found significant at .05 level. Hence, it is concluded that the variables—academic discipline and medium of instruction are not influencing the attitude of academic counsellors towards SSS.

Table 4.5 shows the variable-wise sub-sample means and their comparison of learners.

Table 4.4 : Academic Counsellors Variables

		N	Mean	S.D.		M.D.	$S.E_d$	C.R.
Academic Counsellors	(a) Arts	23	127.8	10.89	a–b	1.4	3.54	0.4
Discipline-wise	(b) Commerce	14	129.2	13.23	b–c	2.5	4.45	0.56
	(c) Science	17	126.7	11.12	c–a	1.1	3.53	0.31
Medium of Instruction	English	14	129.3	12.39		2.5	3.82	0.65
	Telugu	36	126.8	11.46				

Both variables are not significant.

Table 4.5 : Learners Variables

Variables		*N*	*Mean*	*S.D.*	*M.D.*	*S.E$_d$*	*C.R.*
Sex	Men	49	127.5	11.58			
					0.8	2.37	0.34
	Women	53	128.3	12.38			
Employment Status	Employed	38	118.6	14.36			
					6.7	2.83	2.36*
	Unemployed	64	125.3	12.87			
Age	Below 25	19	125.5	11.52 (a–b)			
					6.2	2.95	2.1*
	Between 26 – 45	75	119.3	11.22 (b–c)			
					9.0	4.96	1.8
	Above 45	8	118.3	13.15 (c–a)			
					2.8	5.32	0.53
Academic Discipline	Arts	57	125.3	10.69 (a–b)			
					0.5	2.4	0.21
	Commerce	38	124.6	11.88 (b–c)			
					6.6	3.75	1.78
	Science	17	118.2	13.27 (c–a)			
					7.1	3.5	2.03*
Medium of Learning	English	18	125.3	12.19			
					6.6	3.12	2.11*
	Telugu	84	118.7	11.25			

* C. R. Value significant at 0.05 level. Four learner variables are significant.

As can be seen four of the C. R. values are found significant at .05 level. The concerned variables are employment status, age of the learner, academic discipline and medium of learning.

It appears to be reasonable to conclude that unemployed learners hold a more positive attitude towards SSS. Age as a variable has its influence. Learners below the age of 25 hold a more positive attitude.

Discipline or arts students hold a more favourable attitude than science students. Similarly students with English as medium of learning hold more favourable attitude than students learning through Telugu medium.

Conclusion

The above analysis of data led the investigator draw the following conclusions:

1. The sample of counsellors and learners from two study centres hold a positive attitude towards the SSS.

   Nearly 98 per cent of the counsellors and 90 per cent of the learners are identified as possessing positive attitude.

2. The counsellors hold a more favourable attitude than learners.

3. As far as learners were concerned the variables age, academic discipline, medium of learning and employment status are associated with their attitude towards SSS.

   (a) Young learners, that is learners below the age of 25 hold a more favourable attitude.

   (b) Unemployed learners hold more positive attitude.

   (c) Science students hold comparatively less favourable attitude towards SSS than arts students.

   (d) Learners whose medium of learning is English hold a more favourable attitude than Telugu medium students.

4. The samples of counsellors and learners while expressing positive attitude towards most of the statements, express dissatisfaction about the following:

(a) While expressing satisfaction on aspects of instructional organization, a need for revision of course material is felt.

(b) There is unanimity about the opinion that the course material do not reach the learner in time.

(c) The learners feel that there is a need for considering student need and the course material should be made suitable to the level of students.

(d) A need for increasing the number of counselling days is felt. At the same time the quality of counselling is identified as satisfactory.

(e) The learners expressed the need for making facilities accessible especially the library facilities.

(f) While the importance and quality of assignments was acknowledged, the counsellors felt that the learner does not feel the importance of assignments. They also expressed a need for training in proper evaluation of assignments.

(g) The learners feel the need for making self evaluation through assignments.

(h) Both the samples have acknowledged the importance of evaluation procedures. They feel the need for continuous and comprehensive evaluation which may be taken into consideration for awarding degrees.

Discussion and Suggestions

The Open University system is not just a multi-media approach for teaching distant learners. Its main aim is to equalise educational opportunities and provide open access to higher education for all those disadvantaged groups who could not or did not join the formal stream. While it has distinctive character because of its objectives, operations and spatial needs, it attempts to democratise higher education and does away with the conventional restrictions of place, time and entry qualifications.

The successful functioning of Open University is directly

dependent upon the SSS provided to the learners. The instructional organization, facilities, assignments and evaluation procedures constitute the basic structure of SSS. The focus of the study was attitudes and reactions of teacher and taught towards the above aspects.

On the basis of analysis of data and conclusions the investigator has the following suggestions to improve the quality of SSS:

1. Though this is a preliminary study it has pointed out that the counsellors and learners hold the positive attitude towards the existing SSS. This by itself is significant because it speaks of the general quality of the SSS provided by Dr. B. R. Ambedkar Open University.
2. The employed learners seem to be in need of more assistance through SSS.
3. The library facilities are in need of improvement. Though the English medium students are satisfied, Telugu medium students seem to be requiring better library facilities. A separate study in terms of the library facilities may be taken up.
4. Another opinion to be considered is regarding the periodic revision of course material. The structural organization of the course material may be in terms of self-evaluation procedures. Self instructional modules may be prepared along with assignments.
5. The importance of assignments was acknowledged by the sample and some attempts to improve the quality of assignments is necessary. The suggestion to evolve a comprehensive evaluation system incorporating an internal assessment through assignments is worth considering.
6. Learners have complaint that the course material is not reaching in time. Improving the procedures for supplying the course materials is necessary. Proper time schedules in organizing the instruction and examination will be helpful.

Suggestions for Further Research

1. A detailed study of the problems of learners in terms of employment status and age may yield useful information.
2. A study of the existing audio-visual facilities at study centres may be taken up.
3. An investigation of problems of academic counsellors in adopting the evaluation procedures may serve a useful purpose.
4. A comparative study of SSS among different Open Universities may result in useful data.

5
Summary

Introduction

The University Education Commission (1948–49) remarked: "In a well planned educational system opportunities will be provided at every level to the pupils for the exercise of their reflective powers, artistic abilities and practical work."

On the basis of observation made by the Planning Commission (1960–65) the matter of creation of alternative channels of higher education was brought to the consideration of Central Advisory Board of Education (CABE).

The Education Commission has recommended, "The opportunities for part time education through programmes like correspondence courses should be expanded as widely as possible and should also include course in Science and Technology."

Distance Education has been defined by several writers like Wedemeyer, Holmberg, Moore, Peters and Keegan, each emphasizing certain aspects of the system.

The Open University System is not just a multi-media approach of teaching to a distant learner. It is a philosophical concept of openness providing higher education to one and all who desire to have it. In the most commonly used sense 'open' refers to an "idea of creating opportunities for study for those debarred from it for whatever reasons be it lack of formal educational attainment or shortage of vacancies, poverty, remoteness, employment or domestic necessities."

The Andhra Pradesh Open University was renamed as Dr. B. R. Ambedkar Open University on the occasion of the centenary birth anniversary of Dr. B. R. Ambedkar in the year 1992.

Objectives of the Dr. B. R. Ambedkar Open University

1. To provide educational opportunities to those who could not, nor one reason or another, to take advantage of those offered by the other institutions of higher learning.
2. To realize equality of educational opportunity for as large a number of people as possible including those in employment, house-wives and other adults who wish to upgrade their education or to acquire knowledge and studies in various fields through distance education.
3. To provide flexibility with regard to eligibility for enrolment, age of entry, choice of courses, methods of learning, conduct of examinations and implementation of educational programmes.
4. To formulate programmes complementary to those of existing universities in the State so as to maintain the highest standards on par with those of the best universities in the country.
5. To promote integration within the State through its policies and programmes.
6. To offer Degree Courses and Non-Degree Certificate courses for the benefit of the working population in various fields and those who wish to enrich their lives by studying subjects of cultural or aesthetic values.
7. To make provision for research and for the advancement and dissemination of knowledge.

The organizational structure of the university is similar to that of the other universities in the State though a few changes have been made in its structure to suit the character of the university.

A flexible instructional system is basic to the concept of an Open University. Dr. B. R. Ambedkar Open University has adopted an integrated media approach, in the form of print materials, broadcasting and audio-visual aids, supported by tutorial system, contact classes and summer schools.

Student Support Services

To enable the students to have regular contacts with the university, study centres have been established, 85 in number and located in each district of the State and the twin cities of Hyderabad and Secunderabad, including one in Central Jail. The study centres are located in the existing educational institutions and normally function on all holidays and Sundays and in the evenings on working days.

Each study centre is headed by a Deputy Director/Assistant Director/Co-ordinator who arranges contact-cum-counselling programmes for the students admitted into it and avails itself of the services of the members of the staff of local universities/ colleges on part-time basis. The contact programmes are meant for discussion of the study materials supplied to the students.

Need and Significance of the Study

Dr. B. R. Ambedkar Open University based on the concept of 'Open Learning' the university represents a unique system of realizing the democratization of higher education and the ideal of 'continuing education'. The setting up of Dr. B. R. Ambedkar Open University the first of its kind in the country will go a long way in extending educational opportunities to people in all walks of life without any restriction based on age, sex, occupation or residential situation.

This open university is visualized with great expectations to encourage, strengthen and democratise higher education with flexible methods. Its instruction was through multi-media approach. In this case the success depends mainly on instructional organization or methods that are in use. The open university keeping in view the characteristics of distance education learners, it has planned a well developed student support services in order to clarify their academic problems. If student support services are not maintained well, the students may face problems to continue with their studies.

For effective meet out of these student support services, Academic Counsellors play an important role through study centres for the benefit of the students. Hence there is a need to take up as study, the Student Support Services of Dr. B. R. Ambedkar Open University.

It is also necessary for assessing the extent to which the student support services are really helping students to overcome their problems for successful completion of their courses.

The Present Study

The investigator would like to take up this study to understand student support services of open university, the systematic study of attitudes of Academic Staff and Learners who are involved in preparation to disseminating stage of instructional material and perform other functions at study centres in the forms of student support services.

Learners are real consumers of the student support services of open university. It may be appropriate to include them also in the study to measure their attitudes.

Title of the Study

The title of the present study reads as: "A study of attitudes of Academic Counsellors and Learners towards the Student Support Services of Dr. B. R. Ambedkar Open University."

Objectives of the Study

In accordance with the purposes detailed earlier, the objectives of the present investigation have been specified as:

The objectives of the study are:

1. To identify the attitude of academic counsellors and learners towards Student Support Services (SSS), provided by Dr. B. R. Ambedkar Open University.
2. To identify their reactions towards:

(a) Instructional organization.

(b) Facilities at study centres.

(c) Assignments.

(d) Evaluation procedures.

3. To identify the attitude of academic counsellors in terms of their academic discipline and medium of instruction.
4. To identify the attitude of learners in terms of the following variables i.e., sex, employment status, age, academic discipline and medium of learning.

Delimitation of the Study

The present study is delimited to the academic staff and learners of Dr. B. R. Ambedkar Open University, study centres of Vijayawada and Guntur only.

METHOD OF INVESTIGATION

There are many ways and means of gathering, analysing and reporting research data.

After going through various previous investigations and research papers published on the subject, the researcher constructed an attitude scale consisting of four areas related to SSS. The preliminary tool consisted of 62 items. For identifying the attitude Likert Scaling was adopted and the sample was asked to respond on three point scale.

The tool aimed at measuring attitude of academic counsellors and learners towards SSS of Dr. B. R. Ambedkar Open University on the following areas namely:

1. Regarding instructional organization of Open University.
2. Regarding the facilities at Study Centres.
3. Assignments.
4. Evaluation procedures followed at Open University.

Pilot Study

In order to finalize the statements in the attitude scale, the pilot study was conducted on the sample of 50 comprising of 15 academic counsellors and 35 learners. For this total sample chi-square values for items in the attitude scale were calculated and interpreted at .05 level.

Administration of the Tool

Three hundred questionnaires got prepared for the purpose of this study. Much care was taken to get the questionnaire printed correctly and neatly. Then they were personally handed over to the academic counsellors and learners. Due regard was given for subject-wise and medium of instruction-wise as variables.

Altogether 100 questionnaires each for academic counsellors at two centres were given.

The final questionnaire was given to a sample of 100 learners of Vijayawada study centre at Siddhartha Arts College and another 100 to students of Hindu College, Guntur centre.

Sample

The sample for this investigation consisted of 54 academic counsellors of the study centres of Vijayawada and Guntur.

The learner sample for this investigation was 102 from both the centres.

In both the centres the population of learners was around 2000. The questionnaire was administered to random sample of learners totalling 102 i.e., 5 per cent of the population was contacted by random sampling.

Similarly the population of academic counsellor is around 120 and 54 academic counsellors was contacted i.e., around 45 per cent of the academic counsellors.

The Scoring Procedure

The questionnaire was administered on a three point scale showing agreement, undecided and disagreement with each statement. For identifying the attitude of the sample weighted score technique was adopted and item mean scores were computed.

Weightage given are agreement 3 points, undecided 2

points and disagreement 1 point.

The formula for item mean score is:

$$\text{Item Mean Score} = \frac{\text{Weightage Score}}{N}$$

DATA, CONCLUSIONS AND SUGGESTIONS

Student Support Services (SSS) play an important role in the process of Distance Education. This study of the attitude of counsellors and learners attempts to identify the nature of attitude held by them towards SSS.

Conclusions

The above analysis of data led the investigator draw the following conclusions:

1. The sample of counsellors and learners from two study centres hold a positive attitude towards the SSS.

   Nearly 98 per cent of the counsellors and 90 per cent of the learners are identified as possessing positive attitude.

2. The counsellors hold a more favourable attitude than learners.
3. As far as learners were concerned the variables age, academic discipline, medium of learning and employment status are associated with their attitude towards SSS.
   (a) Young learners, that is learners below the age of 25 hold a more favourable attitude.
   (b) Unemployed learners hold more positive attitude.
   (c) Science students hold comparatively less favourable attitude towards SSS than arts students.
   (d) Learners whose medium of learning is English hold a more favourable attitude than Telugu medium students.
4. The samples of counsellors and learners while expressing positive attitude towards most of the statements, express dissatisfaction about the following:

(a) While expressing satisfaction on aspects of instructional organization, a need for revision of course material is felt.

(b) There is unanimity about the opinion that the course material do not reach the learner in time.

(c) The learners feel that there is a need for considering student need and the course material should be made suitable to the level of students.

(d) A need for increasing the number of counselling days is felt. At the same time the quality of counselling is identified as satisfactory.

(e) The learners expressed the need for making facilities accessible especially the library facilities.

(f) While the importance and quality of assignments was acknowledged, the counsellors felt that the learner does not feel the importance of assignments. They also expressed a need for training in proper evaluation of assignments.

(g) The learners feel the need for making self-evaluation through assignments.

(h) Both the samples have acknowledged the importance of evaluation procedures. They feel the need for continuous and comprehensive evaluation which may be taken into consideration for awarding degrees.

Discussion and Suggestions

On the basis of analysis of data and conclusions the investigator has the following suggestions to improve the quality of SSS:

1. Though this is a preliminary study it has pointed out that the counsellors and learners hold the positive attitude towards the existing SSS. This by itself is significant because it speaks of the general quality of the SSS provided by Dr. B. R. Ambedkar Open University.

2. The employed learners seem to be in need of more assistance through SSS.

3. The library facilities are in need of improvement. Though the English medium students are satisfied, Telugu medium students seem to be requiring better library facilities. A separate study in terms of the library facilities may be taken up.
4. Another opinion to be considered is regarding the periodic revision of course material. The structural organization of the course material may be in terms of self evaluation procedures. Self-instructional modules may be prepared along with assignments.
5. The importance of assignments was acknowledged by the sample and some attempts to improve the quality of assignments is necessary. The suggestion to evolve a comprehensive evaluation system incorporating an internal assessment through assignments is worth considering.
6. Learners have complaint that the course material is not reaching in time. Improving the procedures for supplying the course materials is necessary. Proper time schedules in organising the instruction and examination will be helpful.

Suggestions for Further Research

1. A detailed study of the problems of learners in terms of employment status and age may yield useful information.
2. A study of the existing audio-visual facilities at study centres may be taken up.
3. An investigation of problems of academic counsellors in adopting the evaluation procedures may serve a useful purpose.
4. A comparative study of SSS among different Open Universities may result in useful data.

Bibliography

Amrik Singh, How to train Teachers: A Role for the Open University, India International Centre, Seminar on Open Learning System, Concept and Future, January, 1987.

An Introduction to the Open University, The Open University, Walton Hall, Milton Keynes, 1978.

A Manual for Academic Counsellors, Regional Services Division, IGNOU, New Delhi, 1988.

Bakhshish Singh, Open Teaching Learning System and the Indian Scenario, India International Centre—Seminar on Concept and Future, January, 1987.

Bakhshish Singh, Student Support Services, National Conference on Distance Education, Jointly organised by AIU IGNOU, 9–10 November, 1986, Ahmedabad.

Bhaskara Rao, D., ed., Encyclopaedia of Education for All, 5 Vols., APH Pub. Corporation, New Delhi, 1996.

Bhaskara Rao D., V. V. Rao and V. V. Krishna, Distance Education in Different Countries, Discovery Publishing House, New Delhi, 2000.

Biswal B. N., A Study of Correspondence Education in Indian Universities, An unpublished Ph. D. Thesis, CASE, M. S. University, Baroda.

Desmond Keegan, The Foundation of Distance Education, Croom Helm Ltd., Provident House, Burul Row, Beckenham, Kent BR3 IAT.

Deshmukh K. G., Genesis and the Growth of Distance Education, University News, Special issue, A. U. Publication, November, 1986.

Dutt R., Planning and Development of Distance Education, Journal of Higher Education, Vol. 9, No. 8, Spring, 1984.

Ediger Marlow and D. Bhaskara Rao, Science Curriculum, Discovery Publishing House, New Delhi, 1996.

Ediger, Karlow and D. Bhaskara Rao, Teaching Reading Successfully, Discovery Publishing House, New Delhi, 2000.

Education in Asia, Open University and Distance Education, Quarterly Journal, Ministry of HRD, Govt. of India, Vol. VI, July, August, September, 1986.

Gandhi O. A., Student Support Services for Distance Education: The Indian Context, National Conference on Distance Education, Jointly organised by A. U. & IGNOU, 9–10 November, 1986, Ahmedabad.

Greville Rumble, The Planning and Management of Distance Education, Croom Helm Ltd., Kent, 1986.

Hand Book of Distance Education, AIU House, 16, Kotla Marg, New Delhi, 1986.

Indira Gandhi National Open University, Project Report, September, 1985, New Delhi.

Jeyraj K. V., Student Support Services and Evaluation Methodology, National Conference on Distance Education, Jointly organised by AIU & IGNOU, 9–10 November, 1986, Ahmedabad.

John Coffey, Open Learning Opportunities for Mature Students, UNESCO Press, 1975.

Jose Chander N., Open Learning System, The Concept India International Centre Seminar on Open Learning System, Concept and Future, January 13–14, 1987.

Kumar S., Evaluation Procedures in Distance Education—A Perspective National Seminar on Distance Education, CASE, M. S. University, Baroda, 1987.

Lakshmi T. K. S., Yadav M. S., Ray S., Distance Education in India: Concepts, Possibilities and Issues, National Seminar on Distance Education, CASE, M. S. University, Baroda, 1987.

Marja, Talvi and D. Bhaskara Rao, Educational Leadership and Social Changes, Discovery Publishing House, 1997.

National Policy on Education—1986, Programme of Action, Ministry of Human Resource Development, Government of India, August, 1986.

Narayana Reddy C., Distance Education and Experience of Dr. B. R. Ambedkar Open University, International Seminar, 20–22 November, 1985, New Delhi.

Open University : The Basic Ideas, Sir Walter Perry, The Open University, Walton Hall, Milton Keynes, 1976.

Paramaji: Open University, A Conceptual Analysis, Distance Education, Sterling Publications, New Delhi, 1984.

Perry W., Open University: A Personal Account by the First Vice-Chancellor, The Open University Press, Milton Keynes, 1976.

Prasanth Kumar J. and Digumarti Bhaskara Rao, Effectiveness of Distance Education System, Discovery Publishing House, New Delhi, 1998.

Rathaiah L. and D. Bhaskara Rao, International Innovations in Education, Discovery Publishing House, 1997.

Ram Reddy G., Indira Gandhi National Open University : Its Role in Higher Education, International Seminar on Distance Education, 20–22 November, 1985.

Ram Reddy G., Dr. B. R. Ambedkar Open University, Some New Reflections University News, Special Issue, National Conference on Distance Education, 9–10 November, 1986.

Report of the Education Commission, 1964–66, Government of India, New Delhi.

Report of the Working Group on National Open University (Chairman G. Parthasarathi), Government of India, New Delhi, 1975.

Research on Distance Education in India—A Review, Research on Planning and Management of Distance Education and Educational Technology, April 1988, NIEP & A, New Delhi.

Ruhela S. P., Characteristics of Learners of Distance Education in India, National Seminar on Distance Education, CASE, M. S. University, Baroda, 1987.

Sahea P. K., A Study of Correspondence Education in an Indian University, An unpublished Ph. D. Thesis, CASE, M. S. University, Baroda, 1985.

Sahoo P. K., Researches in Distance Education in India : A Trend Report, Educational Technology Year Book, 1988. Edt. by M. Mukhapadhyay, All India Association for Educational Technology, New Delhi.

Sahoo P. K., Bhat V. D., Students' Attitude Towards Correspondence System of Education, Journal of Indian Education, Volume 13, No. 2, July, 1987, NCERT.

Sneha Joshi M., Student Support Services for Distance Education, University News, Special Issue, National Conference on Distance Education, 9–10 November, 1986.

Sansanwal D. N., Instructional Materials in Distance Education, National Conference on Distance Education, Jointly Organised by AIU & IGNOU, 9–10 November, 1986, Ahmedabad.

Srinivasan T. R., Instructional System of Open University, Assistant Regional Director, IGNOU, Bangalore.

Sudama G. R., Govinda R., Organisation of Distance Education Learning Programmes in India: A Pragmatic Perspective, National Seminar on Distance Education, CASE, M. S. University, Baroda.

Sundara Rao P., Some Problems of Distance Learners, The Progress of Education, Vol. LXII, No. 1, August, 1987.

Towards an Open Learning System/Report of the Committee on the Establishment of an Open University, Hyderabad, A. P., August, 1982.

Tony Dodds, Administration of Distance Teaching Institutions, International Extension College, 1983.

Appendices

APPENDIX 'A'

"A STUDY OF ATTITUDES OF ACADEMIC COUNSELLORS AND LEARNERS TOWARDS THE STUDENT SUPPORT SERVICES OF DR. B. R. AMBEDKAR OPEN UNIVERSITY"

PILOT QUESTIONNAIRE

Please fill in the following particulars:

I. For Academic Counsellors

(a) Name

(b) Subject you are teaching:

(c) Medium of instruction:

II. For learners

(a) Name :

(b) Age in Years :

(c) Whether employed or unemployed :

(d) Degree being studied :

(e) Medium of Learning :

Instructions

Given below are the statements. Please read each statement carefully. To enable you to make your responses easily and quickly, a scale has been provided. Please encircle on the scale following each item the symbol which best indicates your opinion.

The symbols stand for the following:

A – Agree U – Undecided D – Disagree

Regarding Instructional Organisation of Open University

1. Involvement of personnel is not at all according to their abilities. A U D
2. Students are satisfied with the academic activity. A U D
3. Student needs are not properly considered in the courses offered at Open University. A U D
4. The course material prepared by Open University in the subjects I handle is not at all adequate. A U D
5. Course materials in some subjects are good. A U D
6. The course materials currently in use don't need any revision. A U D
7. Illustrations in the course materials are satisfactory. A U D
8. Course materials supplied to learners are useful. A U D
9. Students cannot put to use the course materials. A U D
10. Course materials reach the learners in time. A U D
11. Learners are happy because course materials is supplied in time. A U D

Regarding the Facilities at Study Centres of Open University

12. They should be accessible to all. A U D
13. Their accessibility is not an important issue. A U D
14. They have good library facilities. A U D
15. They need to have good Audio-Visual (A. V.) facilities. A U D
16. The A. V. facilities should be immediately improved. A U D
17. The number of instructional days are sufficient. A U D
18. Counselling days are not sufficient. A U D
19. Convenience of counselling days is important. A U D
20. The timings are not suitable to learners. A U D
21. The timings are inconvenient. A U D
22. The quality of counselling is satisfactory. A U D
23. There is no need to improve the quality of present counselling. A U D
24. Counselling should be organized to help students. A U D
25. There is no need to improve the quality of present counselling. A U D
26. Performance by academic counsellors need not change. A U D
27. Academic counsellors are useful. A U D
28. Counsellor is helping the students to solve their academic problems. A U D

Facilities at Personal Contact Programme (PCP) Centres of Open University

29. Physical facilities are satisfactory. A U D

30. P. C. P. is not useful to students. A U D
31. Teachers services during P.C.P. are satisfactory. A U D
32. Most teachers do not find it difficult to clarify the doubts of students. A U D
33. The teacher student rapport during P.C.P. needs improvement. A U D
34. The P.C.P. cannot initiate the learners towards proper learning. A U D
35. It helps students in improving their learning skills. A U D
36. It does not help students to improve their study habits. A U D
37. Suitability of P.C.P. timings to students is important. A U D
38. P.C.P. venues are accessible to learners. A U D

Assignments

39. Their quality needs improvement. A U D
40. Students should be made to submit them regularly. A U D
41. The assignments are not useful to learners. A U D
42. They should be made to feel their importance. A U D
43. Assignment completion is time consuming. A U D
44. The number of assignments given needs to be changed. A U D
45. They are given in terms of instructional goals. A U D
46. They help the students to develop proper learning habits. A U D

47. The Open University assignments cannot help to students in developing proper study skills. A U D

48. The assignments need help students to evaluate themselves. A U D

49. The academic counsellors are not over-burdened with assignment work. A U D

50. Academic counselling does not serve any purpose. A U D

51. They find it very difficult to value the assignments. A U D

52. They need not be trained in proper evaluation of student assignments. A U D

53. Academic counselling is very important in Open University system. A U D

Evaluation Procedures Followed at Open University

54. The evaluation procedures are not at all satisfactory. A U D

55. They should be improved. A U D

56. They should be made useful. A U D

57. The Open University has to adopt modern evaluation procedures. A U D

58. Open University can introduce good evaluation procedures. A U D

59. Evaluation procedures need not be uniform. A U D

60. Evaluation at Open University means passing the University examination only. A U D

61. It should be made comprehensive. A U D

62. Evaluation of assignments is not time consuming process. A U D

APPENDIX 'B'

"A STUDY OF ATTITUDES OF ACADEMIC COUNSELLORS AND LEARNERS TOWARDS THE STUDENT SUPPORT SERVICES OF DR. B. R. AMBEDKAR OPEN UNIVERSITY"

FINAL QUESTIONNAIRE

Please fill in the following particulars:

I. For Academic Counsellors

(a) Name:

(b) Subject you are teaching:

(c) Medium of instruction:

II. For learners

(a) Name:

(b) Age in Years:

(c) Whether employed or unemployed:

(d) Degree being studied:

(e) Medium of learning:

Instructions

Given below are the statements. Please read each statement carefully. To enable you to make your responses easily and quickly, a scale has been provided. Please encircle on the scale following each item the symbol which best indicates your opinion.

The symbols stand for the following :

A – Agree U – Undecided D – Disagree

Regarding Instructional Organisation of Open University

1. Involvement of personnel is according to their abilities. A U D

2. Students are satisfied with the academic activity. A U D
3. Student needs are properly considered in the courses offered at Open University. A U D
4. The course material prepared by Open university is adequate. A U D
5. Course materials are good. A U D
6. The course materials currently in use need no revision. A U D
7. Illustrations in the course materials are satisfactory. A U D
8. Course materials supplied to learners are useful. A U D
9. Students can put to use the course materials. A U D
10. Course materials reach the learners in time. A U D
11. Course materials supplied is suitable to the level of learners. A U D

Study Centres of Open University

12. The facilities at study centres are accessible to all. A U D
13. They have good library facilities. A U D
14. They have good audio-visual facilities. A U D
15. The number of instructional days are sufficient. A U D
16. Counselling days are sufficient. A U D
17. Counselling days are convenient. A U D
18. The timings are suitable to learners. A U D
19. The quality of counselling is satisfactory. A U D
20. Counselling helps students. A U D

21. Counsellor is helping the students to solve their academic problems. A U D
22. Physical facilities are satisfactory. A U D
23. P.C.P. is useful to students. A U D
24. Teachers services during P.C.P. are satisfactory. A U D
25. Most teachers do not find it difficult to clarify the doubts of students. A U D
26. The teacher student rapport during P.C.P. is satisfactory. A U D
27. The P.C.P. can initiate the learners towards proper learning. A U D
28. It helps students in improving their learning skills. A U D
29. It helps students to improve their study habits. A U D
30. Suitability of P.C.P. timings to students is important. A U D
31. P.C.P. venues are accessible to learners. A U D

Assignments

32. Students submit them regularly. A U D
33. The assignments are useful to learners. A U D
34. The learner feels the importance of the assignments. A U D
35. Assignments completion is time consuming. A U D
36. Sufficient number of assignments are given. A U D
37. They are given in terms of instructional goals. A U D
38. They help the students to develop proper learning habits. A U D

39. The assignments can help the students in developing proper study skills. A U D

40. The assignments help students to evaluate themselves. A U D

41. The academic counsellors are not over burdened with assignment work. A U D

42. They are trained in proper evaluation of student assignments. A U D

Evaluation at Open University

43. The evaluation procedures are satisfactory. A U D

44. They are useful. A U D

45. Evaluation procedures are uniform. A U D

46. Evaluation at Open University means passing the university examination only. A U D

47. It is comprehensive. A U D

48. Getting good assignment grade is as important as passing final examination. A U D

49. Comprehensive evaluation may be taken into consideration for awarding degrees to students. A U D

50. Evaluation of assignments is not a time consuming process. A U D

Index